The Astrology of Ixion

Pluto's Lawless Brother
Our New Seeker Consciousness

A Dwarf Planet University Publication

Artmedia
4, 101 Britten-Jones Dr
Holt ACT 2615
Australia

The Astrology of Ixion
Pluto's Lawless Brother
Our New Seeker Consciousness
ISBN: 978-0-6458033-3-4

Cover image by astrologer, Karina La Puma
Author of the series, A Toolkit for Awakening
www.soul-source.org

The Astrology of Ixion

Pluto's Lawless Brother
Our New Seeker Consciousness

Alan Clay

A Dwarf Planet University Publication

Contents

New Stars for a New Era

Many astrologers believe that new planets are discovered when we are ready to incorporate the new consciousness represented by that planet into our existing consciousness. We've noticed this with the discovery of Uranus, Neptune and Pluto over the last two hundred years. And with the discovery of twelve more planets in the past twenty years, we're now entering a period of rapid consciousness development.

Our personal consciousness develops within the collective consciousness around us, and we see this personal consciousness mapped out in the personal planets in our chart. These are the planets out to Saturn that are visible to the naked eye, and they talk about facets of our personality that are important in living day-to-day.

When our consciousness is focussed on the inner planets, everything that is important is our feelings, our ideas and values, our agency and the luck and material rewards that these bring us. "You can't take it with you, right?" At this level we tend not to be conscious of the action of the outer planets in our lives.

The inner planets represent aspects of personality, while the outer planets represent aspects of consciousness. So, as each new outer planet is discovered, it represents a new aspect of consciousness that is becoming available to us. The discovery of Uranus brought us intuitive consciousness, the discovery of Neptune, spiritual consciousness, and the discovery of Pluto, psychological consciousness.

So, the discovery of Ixion represents a new aspect of consciousness that we can now uncover in ourselves. Put simply, Ixion is our new *seeker consciousness*, giving us an independent streak and enabling us to be authentic and to follow our bliss. In bravely being ourselves we may tread on some toes and to maintain our independence we need to practice asking for forgiveness afterwards rather than permission before. As we develop spiritually, Ixion encourages us to be a unique expression of ourselves, while being sensitive to both the spoken and the unspoken agreements in our relationships, so we know how far we can go.

However, this new consciousness doesn't kick in automatically, rather we must actively incorporate it into our lives. And, because these outer planets talk of consciousness, how they manifest in our lives depends on our current level of consciousness. Most people on Earth experience the outer planets as unconscious influences and so are unable to be sensitive and adaptable to these esoteric new energies. At this level the outer planets are only perceived when, like Pluto, they barge into our lives in a confrontational way.

As we develop spiritually and consciously on-board these new energies into our lives, they become like guides into new territory, offering us special skills or challenges, depending on the aspects in our chart. At this level, rather than unconscious influences, the outer planets become like a new super-consciousness.

Thus, the discovery of so many new outer planets at one time represents a feast of new types of consciousness that is now available to us. The enlightenment that was only available to select gurus and priests is now available to everyone. But just as the gurus had to practice devoutly to be able to handle this divine power, we also need to work to on-board these new energies consciously in our lives.

Physical and Orbital

One of the main ways we discern the meaning of new planets is to look at their physical and orbital characteristics. It tells us a lot about Saturn, that he has 82 moons, 150 moon-like objects, and rings. The precision required for that speaks of his structuring and limiting principals. Uranus spins with East West poles and rotates around the Sun in the opposite direction from most of the other planets, that's very bohemian.

Ixion is a dwarf planet located in the Kuiper Belt, just beyond Neptune. He is classified as a Plutino because his orbit is very similar to that of Pluto. His orbital period of 251 years is just 3 years longer than Pluto. And, like Pluto, Ixion has an orbit which is inclined to the ecliptic of all the inner-Neptunian planets.

The gravity of the Sun and Neptune pull all the planets between them into a plane called the ecliptic, which represents our consensus reality or our common beliefs. And all the trans-Neptunian planets cut through this plane on an angle. Ixion's inclination of 19 degrees is slightly higher than Pluto's 17.

As a result of their inclination, both Ixion and Pluto spend part of each orbit in the underworld and part above, however they are oriented differently. Both have elongated comet-like orbits, but Pluto's perihelion - the point in the orbit closest to the Sun – is above the ecliptic, while Ixion's is below, meaning that Pluto spends more time in the underworld than Ixion.

And finally, both Ixion and Pluto orbit in a 2:3 gravitational resonance with Neptune, so for every 3 Neptune orbits of the Sun, Ixion completes 2. This means that, although the orbits of Ixion and Neptune cross, the planets never actually come close to one another. Just as Pluto cuts inside Neptune at one point in his orbit, the inclination of Ixion's orbit means that he also cuts inside the orbits of both Pluto and Neptune at one point in his cycle, strengthening his influence in that period. We're coming up to the start of his next swing inside Pluto's orbit in 2034.

Astrological Meaning

So, from these orbital characteristics we can see that Ixion has a Plutonian energy, which cuts through existing systems and consensus reality even more than Pluto, but which works more out in the open and less in the underworld. Where Pluto, at the unconscious level, talks of the monsters we hide in our subconscious because we don't want to deal with them, Ixion talks of the monsters we call into the real world where we have to deal with them.

However, like Pluto, the resonance to Neptune lends a spiritual nature to Ixion's energy. Neptune is our spiritual consciousness, and his discovery almost 200 years ago enabled our individual spiritual practice. No longer do we need the group structure of religions as we each can develop our own faith.

So, Ixion's resonance with Neptune tells us that, as we develop spiritually, we will perceive this underworld energy differently. I suggest that, as we do, Ixion gives us the strength to pursue our spiritual passion... which is what we need to pursue a personal spiritual path in this world, a path which will likely start, as we shall see next in the myth, by accepting our passionate nature.

Myth

Myths transmit knowledge across time and culture, but they have to be reinterpreted for the new time and the new culture. In Greek mythology, Ixion was a king of the Lapiths known for his extreme pride and self-absorption, and for his subsequent eternal punishment.

When Ixion got married, he promised his father-in-law a valuable present, but he never delivered on this promise, so his father-in-law stole some of his horses in retaliation. In response Ixion invited him to a feast and, when he arrived, pushed him onto a bed of burning coals, killing him.

Guilt over this drove Ixion mad and the princes of the neighbouring kingdoms refused him catharsis, which was a public process to cleanse his guilt, because they were so offended by his violation of their strict code of guest-host relations. People had to be able to trust that they wouldn't be killed when they were a guest in someone's house. So, Ixion lived as an outlaw and was shunned.

However, the king of the gods, Zeus, took pity on him and brought him to Olympus and introduced him to the other gods. Showing no appreciation, Ixion grew lustful for Zeus's wife, wasting this second chance at rehabilitation and further violating the implicit agreements in guest-host relations.

Zeus got wind of it and substituted a cloud in the shape of his wife, with whom Ixion mated and through this act he fathered the Centaurs, who are half-horse and half-human. These are the brothers and sisters of Chiron, who was himself fathered a different way. For this act Ixion was expelled from heaven and he was bound with snakes to a burning wheel and sent spinning in hell for all eternity.

Myth Interpretation

Alright, so another pretty heavy myth which needs interpretation for our new time and place. And, because these outer planets talk of consciousness, how they manifest in our lives depends on our current level of consciousness. So, Ixion must be interpreted differently at the unconscious level, if we are on the spiritual path, or at a spiritually evolved level.

At the unconscious level the myth suggests the action of this dwarf planet will involve broken promises and retribution leading to an outcast, outlaw status. And there is the danger that second chances will be wasted through the arousal of base passions, and that repeated failure to learn from mistakes will lead to severe punishment.

Once we're on the spiritual path however, Ixion gives us an authenticity in our passionate spiritual mission, which may involve a violation of existing customs and a resulting catharsis, followed by opportunities for a second chance. At this level we are developing the ability to follow our spiritual passion and learn from our mistakes.

And at the spiritually evolved level he offers us the opportunity to define our own rules and live life on our own terms, while respecting the implicit agreements in our relationships and transmuting our base emotions. When we are sensitive to both the spoken and the unspoken boundaries of others, we know how authentic we can be at each point without crossing the line.

Putting Together the Myth & the Orbital Interpretations – Pluto's Lawless Brother

In the myth Ixion has no sense of right or wrong and he lacks boundaries, but he has a joy in life and an inventiveness which carries him through, until he doesn't learn from his mistakes. So in our charts he can give us the strength to take the tiger by the tail and create change, secure in the knowledge that we have to break some eggs in order to make an omelette.

He represents a passionate lawless energy and, because of his orbital alignment with Pluto, we can think of him as Pluto's lawless brother. When positively placed, Ixion gives us an independent streak which enables us to bend the rules to get things done, and to learn from experience. And when negatively placed, to try and get what we want without regard for others, or for norms, and to waste any second chances we may receive.

At the highest level, Ixion is passionate and spiritual, and able to maintain a personal spiritual path... The myth's all about a passionate personal mission and with the orbital resonance to Neptune at the more enlightened level this can become a spiritual mission, where personal passions can become spiritual paths.

Where Neptune's spirituality is nebulous, Ixion takes that energy and focusses it in a personal spiritual mission which is not afraid to experience both the dark and light sides and go beyond the norms. This is the seeker consciousness of Ixion. We need this sort of independent spiritual passion at this time, because religions are breaking down as a way of focussing that Neptunian energy and we are each needing to find the strength to chart our own spiritual course.

So, Ixion encourages us to develop our authenticity and to follow our bliss, which means committing to do the things that bring us joy and purpose. When we do this, the universe will open doors by presenting opportunities and connections we wouldn't have otherwise found.

As mythologist Joseph Campbell said: *If you follow your bliss, you put yourself on a kind of track that has been there all the while waiting for you, and the life you ought to be living is the one you are living. When you can see that, you begin to meet people who are in the field of your bliss, and they open the doors to you. I say, follow your bliss and don't be afraid, and doors will open where you didn't know they were going to be.*[1]

1 Joseph Campbell and the Power of Myth with Bill Moyers, p120

Sabian Symbol for the Discovery Degree

The Sabian Symbols were channelled by clairvoyant Elsie Wheeler and astrologer Marc Edmund Jones, and they give us rich visual symbols for each degree of the zodiac. We can look at the degree of Ixion when he was discovered like a birth moment. As the new planet arrives in our consciousness, the Sabian Symbol of that degree gives us another pathway to interpret this new astrological energy.

Ixion was discovered at 5 degrees 35 minutes of Sagittarius, and we round this up to find the Sabian Symbol. So, the symbol for 6 degrees Sagittarius is:

A Game of Cricket

Dane Rudhyar sees the keynote of this symbol as: *The development of skill in group-situations testing collective goals.*

Any society is built on the interplay between groups of people, each group united by an at least temporary aim. The individual person within the group is assigned a particular role in the play; and definite rules have to be obeyed. The game teaches not only personal skill, but fairness and cooperation.

Where this symbol is found, the value of making individual-will or ego-will subservient to collective cultural patterns is emphasized. Several symbols belonging to this section relate to games or group rituals, because these are "abstracted" from everyday social behaviour and used as educative means to develop group-consciousness and an individual sense- of responsibility to the group.

Theme: The importance of developing Group Solidarity.[2]

Ixion Interpretation from both the Myth & the Discovery Degree

Group solidarity would appear to be the opposite of an independent streak, but what Ixion is encouraging us to ask is: are the rules we're playing by the right ones? What both the myth and the Sabian symbol for the discovery degree have in common is a focus on the spoken or unspoken rules or agreements in our interpersonal relationships.

---

2 *An Astrological Mandala: The Cycle of Transformations and Its 360 Symbolic Phases* (1973), Dane Rudhyar

The myth focusses on what happens when we abuse those agreements, and the discovery degree talks of the successes when we can work together, based on them. Together I think they are saying that while Ixion does encourage us to strike out in new directions and follow our passion on an individual level, the goal here is to find a new way to play our part in the big social game we are all involved in… and thereby develop the game.

Discovery Events

Another way we can infer the meaning of new planets is to look at events around the time of their discovery which can give us an understanding of the astrological energy of the planet.

Ixion was discovered on 22 May 2001 by a team of American astronomers at the Cerro Tololo Inter-American Observatory in Chile. The discovery formed part of the Deep Ecliptic Survey, a survey conducted by American astronomer Robert Millis to search for Kuiper belt objects located near the ecliptic plane.

Ixion was the second outer dwarf planet to be discovered, after Varuna the year before. The discovery of Ixion supported suggestions that there were other undiscovered large trans-Neptunian objects comparable in size to Pluto, so his discovery heralded the discovery of all the other outer dwarf planets.

Because there were no other dwarf planets discovered in 2001, we can use events throughout the year as discovery events for Ixion.

Wikipedia was launched on the 15th January 2001.

Wikipedia is a free, web-based, collaborative, multilingual encyclopaedia project, which went on to become the largest and by far the most popular general reference work on the Internet. As of early November 2025, the English Wikipedia has approximately 7.09 million articles, while all language editions combined contain over 65 million articles. These have all been written by volunteers from around the world.

We see the seeker consciousness of Ixion in the search for meaning and understanding which is inherent in Wikipedia. And we see the personal passion of Ixion in the volunteer participation. Each person makes their contribution on the topic that they are most passionate about. And together, just like the Sabian Symbol suggests, they are playing a larger dynamic game which is a manifestation of group consciousness.

The Netherlands becomes the first country to legalise same-sex marriage

On 1st April 2001, *The Act on the Opening up of Marriage* went into effect in the Netherlands, which became the first country to legalise same-sex marriage. This milestone reflected a broader shift in societal and cultural attitudes around the world, leading to many other countries enacting similar legislation in the following years. The list had grown to 34 by 2023, with the trend suggesting that a majority of the world's countries would do so by the mid-2040s.

We know the personal sexual passion of Ixion from the myth, so we can see the resonance of the planet with the LGBTQ community and with the campaign to have the right to love who we want to love despite conditioning and social pressure. By following their heart those in the LGBTQ community have found a new way to play their part in the big social game we are all involved in... and thereby they developed the game. Ixion enables us to follow our bliss unapologetically and it is through these personal courageous acts that society changes.

A devastating terror attack leaves 3,000 dead in America

On September 11th, 2001, a series of coordinated suicide attacks took place in the United States. On that day, 19 al-Qaeda terrorists hijacked four commercial airliners. The hijackers intentionally crashed two of them into the Twin Towers of the World Trade Centre in New York City – killing everyone on board, along with many others working in the buildings. The towers, which were two of the tallest in the world at the time, both collapsed within two hours, destroying nearby buildings and heavily damaging others.

Again we can see the resonance of the myth with this discovery event. In the myth Ixion killed his father-in-law because of a dispute about his marriage gift, and we see a similar willingness to kill because of a grievance in these al-Qaeda terrorists. This is Ixion at the unconscious level, where we are so self-involved and intent on satisfying our primal desires, that casualties are immaterial.

We can see in this event that Pluto's lawless brother can encourage us to go to any extreme, and take advantage wherever we can, to fulfill our base desires. And we see the seeker consciousness of Ixion in the al-Qaeda ideology which lies behind these actions. They weren't just mindless actions, but rather the result of a new way of thinking about the fundamentalist ideas that gave rise to them.

When we study Ixion in charts, we do see it manifesting, in the extreme, as selfish, seemingly wicked actions taken by people or groups to further their personal agenda. And it is important to realise that it doesn't look that way to them. So in our personal lives, when we take action to further our personal agenda, we likely won't experience that as wicked. But we always have to ask ourselves, "Are our actions self-serving and taken without regard for the consequences?" And we have to be sensitive to the rules in our relationships so we know how far we can go.

We have both spoken and unspoken rules in all our social interactions, and we know from the Sabian Symbol that Ixion brings up the question "are the rules we're playing by the right ones?" It's obvious that you don't fly a plane into a building because of the damage and loss of life that would cause, so this is an unspoken rule. Unless, of course, that is the effect you want.

So, Ixion is constantly pushing us to reconsider our assumptions in our interactions and be sensitive to the agreements that we have with others. As a result of this event rules were changed. Today we have improved security protocols, enhanced global cooperation against terrorism, greater emphasis on emergency preparedness, and increased community unity and resilience.

Apple launches the iPod

And finally, the iPod was a new line of portable media players designed and marketed by Apple Inc, which morphed into the iPhone 6 years later. The first generation was launched on 10th November 2001. With its user-friendly interface and gigabytes of storage capacity, the iPod went on to become phenomenally successful. And the introduction of the iTunes store, with millions of songs available to download, substantially boosted Apple's fortunes.

The freedom to take your personal musical eco-system with you wherever you go is part of the passion and authenticity of Ixion. Our musical library provides the context and a soundtrack for our individuality. It helps articulate who we are and, as we hear it, our authenticity is reinforced. Our soundtrack connects the events in our lives together, underpinning each in the way that a film score supports the drama.

Astrological Meaning

So, let's pull the astrological meaning of this new planet together. Ixion opens us to seeker consciousness, allowing us to develop our authenticity and to follow our bliss. We are one with the universe, but still exist as an individual, and that dichotomy is bridged by being authentically ourselves in our contact with each moment and with the divine.

Ixion is the wild child in each of us that just wants to satisfy our personal passions and is constantly asking *'Are the rules we're playing by the right ones?'* He teaches us to foster an independence of spirit, which enables our seeker consciousness and allows us to pursue a personal spiritual mission.

He gives us the passion to be authentically ourselves and in doing so we will likely step outside the norm and push the social envelope. In bravely being ourselves, we may step on some toes and, to maintain our freedom of action, we need to practice asking for forgiveness afterwards, rather than permission before.

In myth Ixion has no sense of right or wrong and he lacks boundaries. What he does have is an inventiveness and a joy in life. So in our lives he gives us the strength to follow our bliss, even if it means taking the tiger by the tail to create change. We can do this secure in the knowledge that we have to break some eggs in order to make an omelette.

To enable this energy in our lives, we need to own the 'bad' girl or 'bad' boy inside us. Society and our upbringing have labelled certain things or actions bad, to guide us away from them, but they are likely just repressed energies that have been given a negative label. So the 'bad' boy or girl inside is like being ourselves without these inhibitions.

The secret to releasing these inhibitions is to become sensitive to the unspoken agreements in our relationships. Then we can sense how far we can go in each interaction. We have unspoken agreements with everyone, even strangers we pass on the sidewalk: we unconsciously agree not to touch them or look in their eyes. These agreements are different for everyone, and the grey area between our inhibitions and the unspoken agreements is Ixion's play-space.

At the personal planet level of consciousness, Ixion compulsively urges us to disregard boundaries and take what we want when we want it, without any consideration for others. This is obviously going to lead us into trouble, which we overlook in the passion of the moment. As a result of this, we may not keep our promises, which can lead to retribution and eventually to an outcast, outlaw status.

Once outcast, we may receive a second chance and we have to embrace that opportunity and learn from our experience, so we don't repeat our mistakes. However, at this level there is the danger that we will waste our second chance through the arousal of base passions. So, when we are unconscious of this energy, we may try and get what we want without regard for norms and waste any second chances we may receive.

Once we're on the spiritual path, however, Ixion represents a passionate spiritual mission which may involve a violation of existing customs and a resulting catharsis, followed by opportunities for a second chance. At this level, we can embrace the freedom to be ourselves, to forgive our missteps and learn from our mistakes.

As we develop spiritually, our seeker consciousness is enabled, and this gives us the strength to pursue our personal spiritual passion. This new consciousness is what we need to pursue a personal spiritual path in this world, a path which will likely start by accepting our passionate nature. At this level, Ixion represents a passionate lawless energy with an ability to bend the rules to get things done and to learn from experience.

As we reach the spiritually evolved level, we can define our own rules and live life on our own terms, while respecting the implicit agreements in our relationships and transmuting our base emotions. At this level, Ixion is passionate and spiritual, and able to maintain a personal spiritual path. The myth is all about a passionate personal mission and, with the orbital resonance with Neptune, at the more enlightened level this can become a spiritual mission, where personal passions can become spiritual paths.

Where Neptune's spirituality is nebulous, Ixion takes that energy and focusses it in a personal spiritual mission that is not afraid to experience both the dark and light sides and to go beyond the norms. We need a strong internal passion to guide us beyond the traditional ideas that are crumbling around us in the present era. Our world and our place in it are changing so fast that the old rules don't work effectively anymore, and we each need to develop our seeker consciousness to chart our own course into the future.

Owning our Bad Boy or Bad Girl

As with all the planetary energies, when we don't own the energy, we project it out into our lives and then we will call bad boys and bad girls to us. We need this energy of 'pushing the boundaries' in our lives so either we own it, or we attract it. And when we attract it we have no control over how it manifests. Generally, it will manifest as undesirable people coming into our lives in the area associated with our Ixion house placement. For those experiencing this, see Exercise 3 below.

And a quick reminder of the cautionary tale of the myth, for those who think that, because we need to let our bad person out, we can just do anything we want. Think again. If we want to avoid punishing consequences, we need to be sensitive about following our passion right up to the line, and if we cross it, learning from our mistake so it doesn't happen again. We need to be sensitive to both the spoken and unspoken agreements we have with others, so we know how authentic we can be in each situation.

Ixion Consciousness Challenges

We see in our research at the Dwarf Planet University, how, by simply making these new planets conscious, students become empowered, and their lives are transformed. To do this we need to engage with these new consciousness energies, and by engaging, we take them out of the unconscious arena of action.

To enable this engagement, here are some consciousness challenges for Ixion. These are exercises to help you engage with this new aspect of consciousness, so you can on-board his energy in your life. As you do, you will find yourself becoming empowered and your life will be transformed.

1. Follow your bliss. If you don't normally follow your heart, make an effort to *spontaneously* do something you really want to do, *when you want to do it*. The secret is to 'give yourself permission'. One way to do this is to declare a holiday and give yourself 'time off'.

2. Have a 'bad' person day. Set aside a day where you let yourself do the things you really want to do, but don't normally let yourself. If challenged, practice asking for forgiveness afterwards, rather than seeking permission before.

3. Offing the others. If Ixion is manifesting as disreputable others coming into your life, it means that you are not expressing your 'bad' girl or 'bad' boy energy. Try gradually letting yourself out to play by doing one of the things you secretly long to do. As you own this energy, you will find that there is no need for it to manifest as others pushing you to be authentic.

4. Change the rules. In the area of life represented by your Ixion house position, ask yourself, *"Are the rules I'm playing by, the right ones?"* And if they are not, *"Can any of them be changed?"* Take action to change any that you can.

5. Second time lucky. The more we can learn from our experience, the better. Notice when you encounter a lesson a second time and immediately internalize that lesson, so you don't encounter it a third time. The third time could be the burning wheel.

6. Pushing boundaries. Pay attention to the unspoken agreements in each moment of your day. Each individual is different in their application of the general rules of behavior, and in their tolerance for flexibility. Then, when you feel it's okay, be proactive about pushing the boundaries where it is not going to be a problem.

7. Normal / Abnormal question. Here's an Ixionic street exercise to explore boundaries. Choose a busy pedestrian area and watch the people. They are all different. Many wear their boundaries on the outside and you can tell that they don't want interaction. After a while choose someone who looks approachable and ask them a normal question. *"Can you tell me the time?"* or *"Where is the supermarket?"*. If they tell you and move on, there is an unspoken boundary clicking in. But if they are hanging around and you feel they are open to more, follow that with an abnormal question. *"Do you like dancing?"* or *"What did you eat for breakfast?"*. For some the boundary clicks in then, and they will walk off at that point, while others will play along.

Case Study – Prince Harry

The former Duke of Sussex, Prince Harry, has Ixion exactly conjunct his Midheaven, so he exemplifies the willful 'lawless' social mission of Ixion. As a child he was reportedly referred to by his mother as 'the naughty one' of the family. In his teenage years the press labeled him a 'wild child' when he was seen smoking cannabis, drinking underage and fighting with paparazzi outside nightclubs. More recently he spectacularly resigned from his royal duties to prioritize his wife and family.

His Ixion is also closely conjunct Quaoar, our new planet of spirit consciousness, which enables us to find a practice to bring spirit into mater. As an adult, Harry does have daily yoga and meditation practices, and the conjunction with Ixion brings an authenticity into his spiritual practice which is exemplified in the following review in the Wall Street Journal from January 2023:

Prince Harry's memoir, "Spare," is among other things a spiritual autobiography—a New Age story of suffering and rebirth. Harry has said he's "not religious," but he is spiritual. Christianity leaves him cold, but he pursues enlightenment with a zeal that would have warmed the heart of a Puritan divine. He travels this path alone, guided by drugs, spirit animals sent by his late mother, Diana, and daily yoga and meditation.[3]

His Ixion is also semi-sextile both his Venus on his 9th House cusp and Mars in the 11th House, so his social mission aligns with his values and knowledge and with the actions he takes to affect the collective consciousness and, as a result, he is a leading campaigner for various causes. He campaigns for veterans and service members through organizations like the Invictus Games, and for mental health with his role at BetterUp and the Heads Together campaign.

His Ixion is also quintile Mercury in the 8th House, so his willful social mission enables communication about these collective issues. He is also a strong advocate for children's and youth issues, including support for those affected by HIV/AIDS and for anti-violence initiatives in the UK.

---

3 https://www.wsj.com/articles/prince-harrys-pagan-progress-spiritual-religious-spare-diana-hunting-meghan-markle-faith-millennial-11674166657

Name: ♂ Duke of Sussex Harry [Adb]		
born on Sa., 15 September 1984	Time: 4:20 p.m.	
in Paddington, ENG (UK)	Univ.Time: 15:20	
0w12, 51n32	Sid. Time: 14:58:16	Type: 2.GW 0.0-1 16-Feb-2026

Natal Chart (Method: Web Style / Placidus)
Sun sign: Virgo
Ascendant: Capricorn

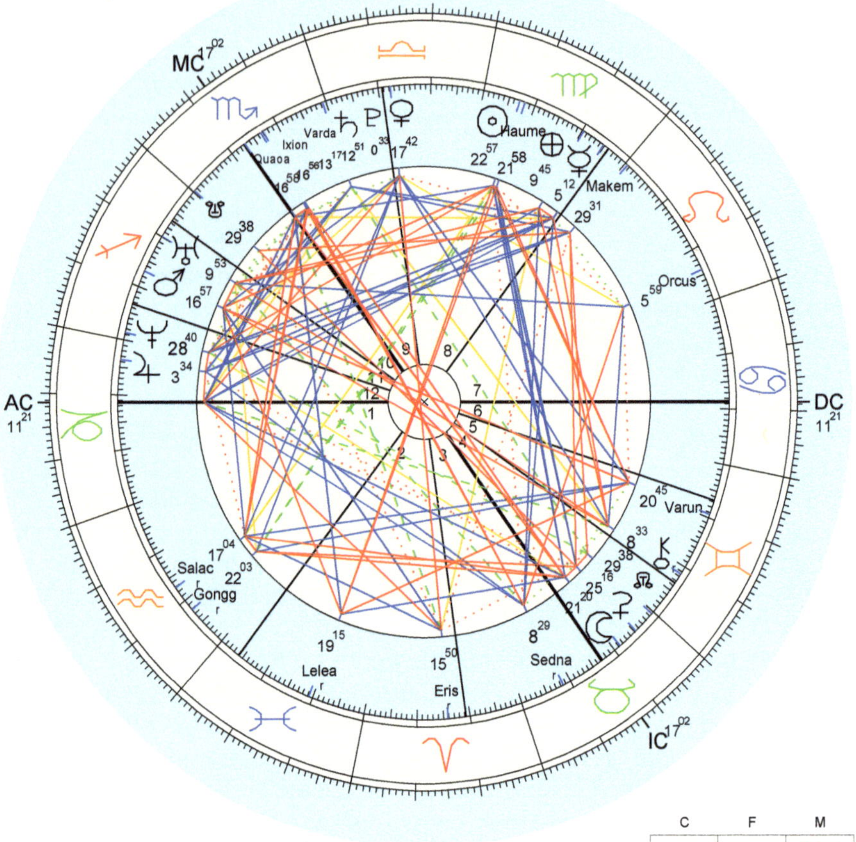

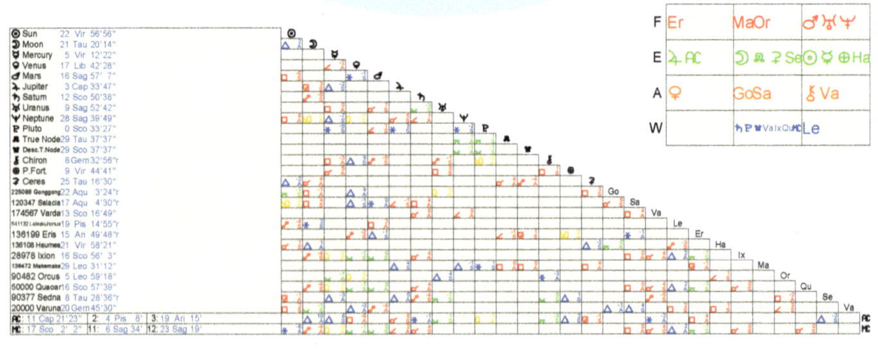

Sun	22 Vir 56'56"
Moon	21 Tau 20'14"
Mercury	5 Vir 12'22"
Venus	17 Lib 42'28"
Mars	16 Sag 57' 7"
Jupiter	3 Cap 33'47"
Saturn	12 Sco 50'38"
Uranus	9 Sag 52'42"
Neptune	28 Sag 39'49"
Pluto	0 Sco 33'27"
True Node	29 Tau 37'37"
Desc.T.Node	29 Sco 37'37"
Chiron	8 Gem 32'56"r
P.Fort.	9 Vir 44'41"
Ceres	25 Tau 16'30"
225088 Gonggong	22 Aqu 3'24"r
120347 Salacia	17 Aqu 4'30"r
174567 Varda	13 Sco 16'49"
541132 Leleakuhonua	19 Pis 14'55"r
136199 Eris	15 Ari 49'48"r
136108 Haumea	21 Vir 58'21"
28978 Ixion	16 Sco 56' 3"
136472 Makemake	29 Leo 31'12"
90482 Orcus	5 Leo 59'18"
50000 Quaoar	16 Sco 57'39"
90377 Sedna	8 Tau 28'36"r
20000 Varuna	20 Gem 45'30"

AC: 11 Cap 21'23"	2: 4 Pis 8'	3: 19 Ari 15'
MC: 17 Sco 2' 2"	11: 6 Sag 34'	12: 23 Sag 19'

	C	F	M
F	Er	MaOr	♂♅♆
E	♃ AC	☽ ☊ ⚳ Se	☉ ☿ ⊕ Ha
A	♀	GoSa	⚷ Va
W		♄ ♇ ☋ Va Ix Qu MC	Le

Transiting Case Study

Harry married Meghan Markle in May 2019 and, just hours before the wedding, his grandmother, Queen Elizabeth II, made him the Duke of Sussex. Then in January 2020, he spectacularly resigned from his royal duties, with the couple announcing their intention to step back as senior members of the royal family and split their time between the UK and North America. Who resigns from being a prince? That's a fairytale role. But we see that with Ixion on the MC, Harry was motivated to ask, "Are the rules I'm playing by the right ones?" And, when he decided that they weren't, to prioritise instead his IC, his home life with his wife and family.

Split Announced

So let's have a look at Harry's transits as the split was announced. The transiting planets show how we are developing the consciousness energies that they represent, and their aspects to natal Ixion talk of that influence on our authenticity. Transiting Ixion meanwhile is talking about our developing authenticity, our developing seeker consciousness.

When the split with the royal family was announced on the 8th January 2020, Harry had the transiting Sun closely sextile his natal Ixion, showing that the move was central to his growing authenticity. This change allowed him to make choices independent of royal constraints, and he repeatedly cited the importance of "living authentically" and making decisions for his family's safety and well-being, as he explained his decision.

Meanwhile transiting Chiron, the Centaur of wounding and healing, and transiting Salacia, our new planet of higher love consciousness, were conjunct, with both closely sesquiquadrate his Ixion. The sesquiquadrate is a square and a half and, while it is normally considered a minor aspect, the dwarf planets orbit so slowly that they sit somewhere by transit for years, strengthening the aspect and the planet's action through consistency.

In myth, Neptune proposed to Salacia because she was so appealing, and she became the goddess of the sparking surface water, so she can bring us a degree of sparkling popularity. Harry has Salacia nataly in the 1st house and he has always been the centre of media attention. So the sesquiquadrate from the transiting Chiron-Salacia conjunction to his natal Ixion, suggests that the split would necessitate some healing in his growth and be controversial with the public, but that his growing authenticity would likely make him more popular. Transiting Neptune was meanwhile closely trine his Ixion in the 10th house, showing his independent social move to be the fulfilment of a dream. And transiting Ixion was simultaneously closely conjunct his natal Neptune in the 12th House, showing the release from the web of influence of the institution of the royal family that the announcement provided.

His natal Neptune is trine Makemake, our new planet of systems consciousness, in his seventh house of relationships, so transiting Ixion was also trine his natal Makemake. Makemake is 'our model of the world and how it works' which we build up through our experience. So Harry's developing seeker consciousness was enabling a deeper understanding of the world and of his place in it, through his

Name: ♂ Duke of Sussex Harry [Adb]		
born on Sa., 15 September 1984	Time: 4:20 p.m.	
in Paddington, ENG (UK)	Univ.Time: 15:20	
0w12, 51n32	Sid. Time: 14:58:16	Type: 2.GW 0.0-1 16-Feb-2026

Natal Chart (Method: Web Style / Placidus)
Sun sign: Virgo
Ascendant: Capricorn
Transits 8 Jan. 2020

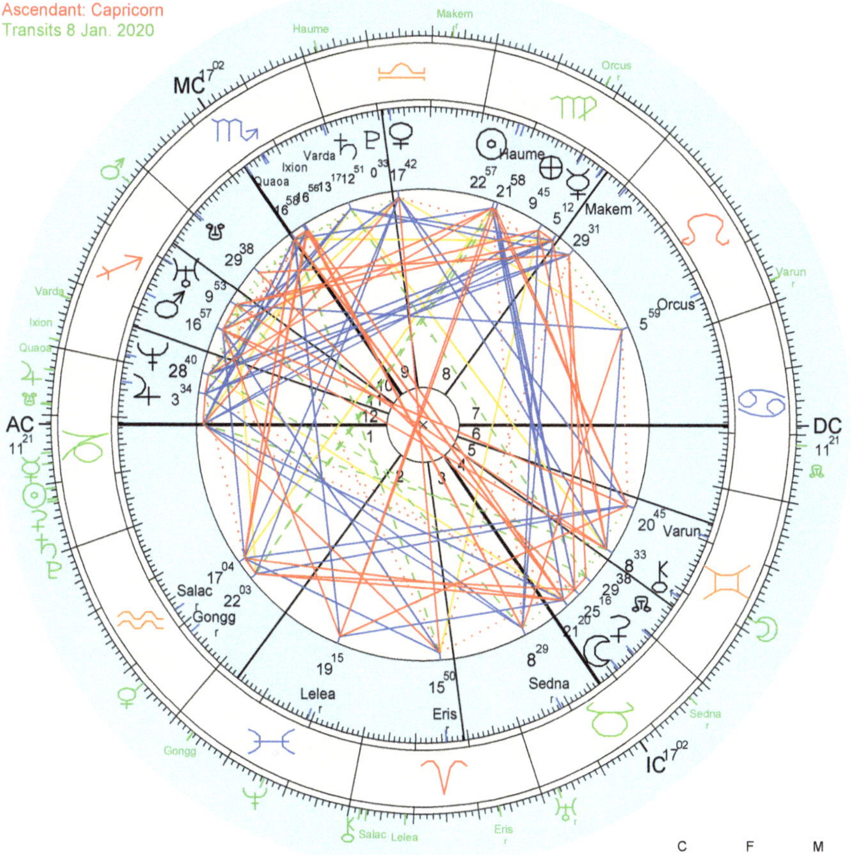

	Natal	Transit
☉ Sun	22 Vir 56'56"	17 ♑ 9'
☽ Moon	21 Tau 20'14"	11 ♊ 47'
☿ Mercury	5 Vir 12'22"	15 ♑ 33'
♀ Venus	17 Lib 42'28"	22 ♒ 58'
♂ Mars	16 Sag 57' 7"	3 ♐ 6'
♃ Jupiter	3 Cap 33'47"	8 ♑ 17'
♄ Saturn	12 Sco 50'38"	22 ♑ 13'
♅ Uranus	9 Sag 52'42"	2 ♉ 39'r
♆ Neptune	28 Sag 39'49"	16 ♓ 25'
♇ Pluto	0 Sco 33'27"	22 ♑ 37'
☊ True Node	29 Tau 37'37"	8 ♋ 26'd
☋ Desc.T.Node	29 Sco 37'37"	8 ♑ 26'd
⚷ Chiron	8 Gem 32'56"r	1 ♈ 44'
⊕ P.Fort.	9 Vir 44'41"	not av.
⚳ Ceres	25 Tau 16'30"	20 ♑ 42'
225088 Gonggong	22 Aqu 3'24"r	3 ♓ 35'
120347 Salacia	17 Aqu 4'30"r	2 ♈ 45'
174567 Varda	13 Sco 16'49"	22 ♐ 35'
541132 Leleakuhonua	19 Pis 14'55"r	8 ♈ 44'
136199 Eris	15 Ari 49'48"r	23 ♈ 13'r
136108 Haumea	21 Vir 58'21"	27 ♎ 47'
28978 Ixion	16 Sco 56' 3"	28 ♐ 56'
136472 Makemake	29 Leo 31'12"	6 ♎ 51'r
90482 Orcus	5 Leo 59'18"	12 ♍ 4'r
50000 Quaoar	16 Sco 57'39"	3 ♑ 23'
90377 Sedna	8 Tau 28'36"r	27 ♉ 2'r
20000 Varuna	20 Gem 45'30"	3 ♌ 16'r

AC: 11 Cap 21'23"	2: 4 Pis 8'	3: 19 Ari 15'
MC: 17 Sco 2' 2"	11: 6 Sag 34'	12: 23 Sag 19'

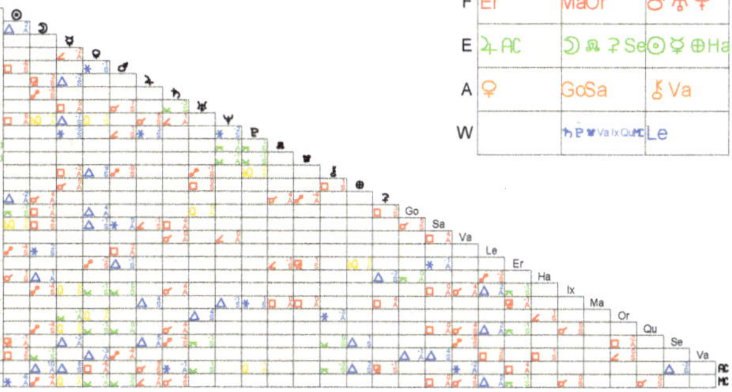

	C	F	M
F	Er	MaOr	♂ ♅ ♆
E	♃ AC	☽ ☊ ⚳ Se	☉ ☿ ⊕ Ha
A	♀	GoSa	⚷ Va
W		♄ ♇ ☋ Va Ix Qu MC	Le

relationships. In California, the couple developed relationships with other activists, celebrities, and advocates, so the split did enable a broadening of his social and professional circle.

Meanwhile transiting Ixion was also closely quintile his natal Venus on his 9th House cusp, showing the opportunity for relationships and travel that his developing authenticity was enabling. The split put immense pressure on both him and Meghan, but by their own accounts, their partnership became more central and resilient. He credits her with challenging his perspectives and supporting his break with royal tradition, and their subsequent public appearances and projects have showcased a collaborative approach.

Transiting Ixion was also inconjunct his natal North Node in the 4th house, showing the split to be both a fated and a destined move to create a sacred space for his family. And this meant that it was semi-sextile his South Node in the 10th house, signalling that it would also help him resolve karma about his place in society.

Split Became Effective

The split became effective on the 31st March 2020 and on this date he had both the transiting Sun and Moon closely bi-quintile his natal Ixion, showing the importance of the move and the opportunity it provided. The bi-quintiles are evolutionary flows which become like super-opportunities when we actively engage with them.

And the transiting North Node in his 6th house was sesquiquadrate his Ixion, so the split was challenging him to find a new way to pursue his destined service. While the transiting South Node in his 12th house was semi-square his Ixion, talking about release of karma and unconscious baggage that the split was enabling. Meanwhile transiting Ixion was still inconjunct his North Node in the 4th House, showing that this was all part of a fateful phase in his destined work to create a sacred space for his family.

Ixion was also transiting sextile his natal Pluto in the 9th House, talking about the freedom he was gaining from being under the thumb of power, and the resulting empowerment that gave him to reach out into the world through publishing and media. Over the next few years he entered into deals to make films with Netflix and publish books with Penguin Random House.

Name: ♂ Duke of Sussex Harry [Adb]
born on Sa., 15 September 1984 — Time: 4:20 p.m.
in Paddington, ENG (UK) — Univ.Time: 15:20
0w12, 51n32 — Sid. Time: 14:58:16

Type: 2.GW 0.0-1 6-Dez-2025

Natal Chart (Method: Web Style / Placidus)
Sun sign: Virgo
Ascendant: Capricorn
Transits 31 Mar. 2020

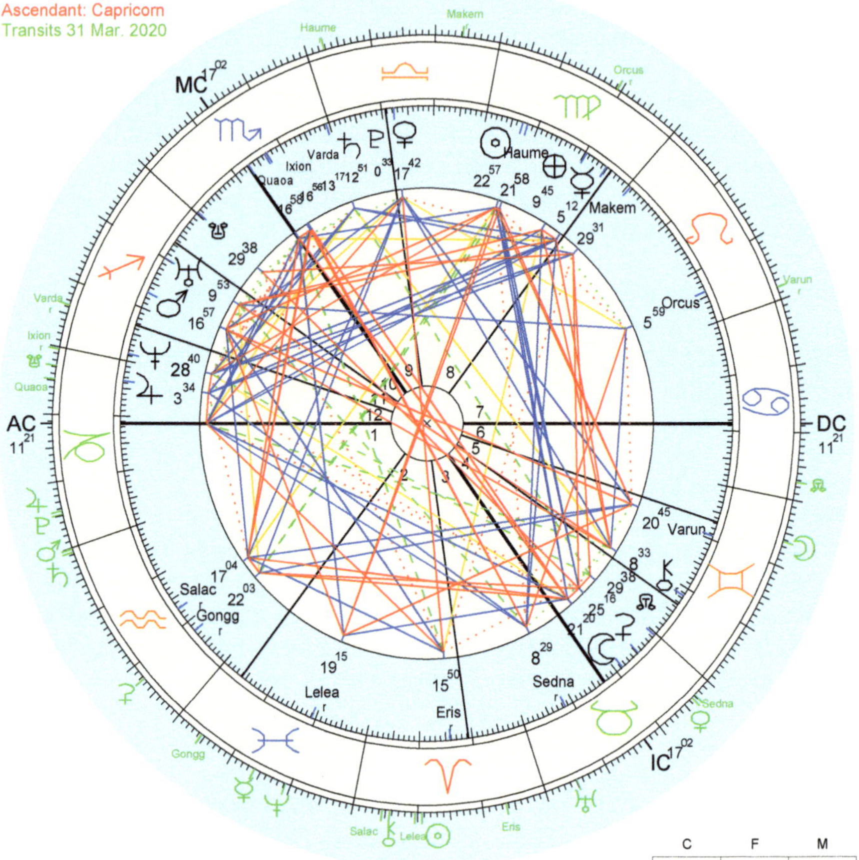

	Natal	Transit
☉ Sun	22 Vir 56'56"	10 ♈ 44'
☽ Moon	21 Tau 20'14"	23 ♊ 49'
☿ Mercury	5 Vir 12'22"	14 ♓ 0'
♀ Venus	17 Lib 42'28"	20 ♉ 35'
♂ Mars	16 Sag 57' 7"	0 ♒ 7'
♃ Jupiter	3 Cap 33'47"	24 ♑ 16'
♄ Saturn	12 Sco 50'38"	0 ♒ 37'
♅ Uranus	9 Sag 52'42"	5 ♉ 7'
♆ Neptune	28 Sag 39'49"	19 ♓ 14'
♇ Pluto	0 Sco 33'27"	24 ♑ 50'
☊ True Node	29 Tau 37'37"	2 ♋ 44'
☋ Desc.T.Node	29 Sco 37'37"	2 ♑ 44'
⚷ Chiron	8 Gem 32'56"r	5 ♈ 41'
⊕ P.Fort.	9 Vir 44'41"	not av.
⚳ Ceres	25 Tau 16'30"	22 ♒ 21'
225088 Gonggong	22 Aqu 3'24"r	4 ♓ 29'
120347 Salacia	17 Aqu 4'30"r	4 ♈ 31'
174567 Varda	13 Sco 16'49"	23 ♐ 35'r
541132 Leleakuhonua	19 Pis 14'55"r	9 ♈ 38'
136199 Eris	15 Ari 49'48"r	23 ♈ 44'
136108 Haumea	21 Vir 58'21"	27 ♎ 9'r
28978 Ixion	16 Sco 56' 3"	0 ♑ 15'r
136472 Makemake	29 Leo 31'12"	5 ♎ 47'r
90482 Orcus	5 Leo 59'18"	10 ♍ 39'r
50000 Quaoar	16 Sco 57'39"	4 ♑ 43'
90377 Sedna	8 Tau 28'36"r	27 ♉ 11'
20000 Varuna	20 Gem 45'30"	1 ♌ 57'r

AC: 11 Cap 21'23"	2: 4 Pis 8'	3: 19 Ari 15'
MC: 17 Sco 2' 2"	11: 6 Sag 34'	12: 23 Sag 19'

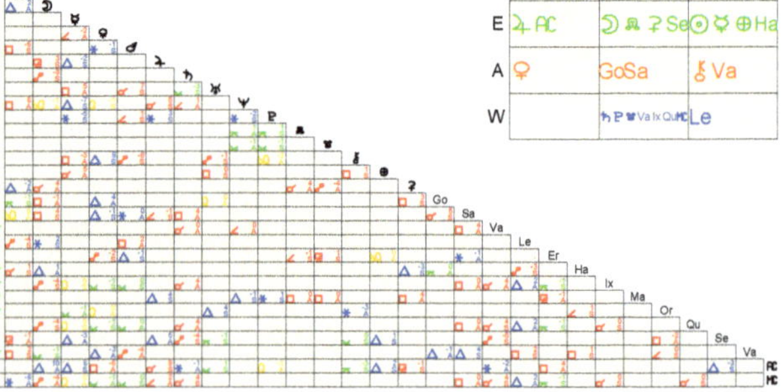

	C	F	M
F	Er	MaOr	♂ ♅ ♆
E	♃ AC	☽ ☊ ⚳ Se	☉ ☿ ⊕ Ha
A	♀	GoSa	⚷ Va
W		♄ ♇ ☋ Va Ix Qu MC	Le

There was also a focus on a rejuvenation of his relationships, with transiting Ixion still quintile his natal Venus on the 9th House cusp, showing how the split was an opportunity for a flowering of his values and his relationships. His work with mental health, personal authenticity, social justice, and protective fatherhood, became more pronounced and actionable after he left his royal duties.

And transiting Ixion was bi-quintile his natal Orcus, our new planet of karmic consciousness, also in the 7th house. Orcus is Pluto's straight talking brother who enables us to align with a creed, to develop our karmic integrity, and at the top level to turn shadow into light. So the split was an evolutionary opportunity for Harry to transmute shadow into light in his one-to-one relationships. His relationships with his father, brother, and other royals became strained through the split, as he documented in his memoir. But he has also described his sense of liberation that he experienced at no longer having to act according to expectations he felt were incompatible with his values.

Finally transiting Ixion was still closely trine his natal Makemake in the 7th house, as he embraced a new understanding of what was possible for him in his one-to-one relationships through the changes he was initiating. Makemake is the higher octave of Uranus and the shift enabled him to forge new supportive networks. It also allowed him to engage more directly with causes he cares about, and it empowered his marriage. His relationships with Megan, his children, and his broader community have deepened since the split, as has his sense of purposeful identity.

Case Study – Gretta Thunberg

Gretta Thunberg is a Swedish climate-change activist who was 15 and had just started ninth grade when she decided not to attend school until the Swedish general election two weeks later to protest climate change. Her protest began after the heat waves and wildfires during Sweden's hottest summer in at least 262 years.

We don't know her time of birth, so I'm using a rectified chart that places Ixion on her MC which is also conjunct her South Node. This conjunction means that she brings a lot of karmic power and a lawless activism to her social role. Her blunt and direct style cuts through political jargon and forces people to confront the urgency and severity of the crisis, making it understandable on a personal level.

She also has Ixion trine Ceres and sextile Neptune, both in a very large 1st House, so as part of the very core of her being she understands the larger vision and the need to nurture the planet and exemplifies this. Her personal protest empowered other young people to believe in their power to create change and to engage in similar protests in their own communities. Together, they organised a school climate strike movement, and global strike a year later gathered more than one million strikers.

Her Ixion is also square her Salacia, our new planet of higher-love consciousness, which is also in her 1st house, so she is able to connect intimately with others, to make the most of her opportunities and develop a light-heartedness which both protects her and enables her appeal. She frequently uses a light-hearted, often sarcastic approach, particularly on social media, which has enabled her posts to go viral.

After she gave a powerful, and at times angry, UN speech, the U.S. President mocked her, calling her a "very happy young girl." She responded by using the quote as her Twitter bio. While her public persona often involves seriousness, her use of light-hearted, humorous tactics is a way to engage with those who might disagree with her and also rally her supporters in a less confrontational way.

And finally, her Ixion is also sextile Haumea, our new planet of unity consciousness, in her 7th house of one-to-one relationships, so she brings rejuvenation and an understanding that we are all in this together into all her interactions. She frames the climate crisis as a moral and urgent

Name: ♀ Gretta Thunberg
born on Fr., 3 January 2003
in Stockholm, SWED
18e03, 59n20

Time: 9:27 a.m.
Univ.Time: 8:27
Sid. Time: 16:29:24

Type: 2.GW 0.0-1 16-Feb-2026

Natal Chart (Method: Web Style / Placidus)
Sun sign: Capricorn
Ascendant: Capricorn

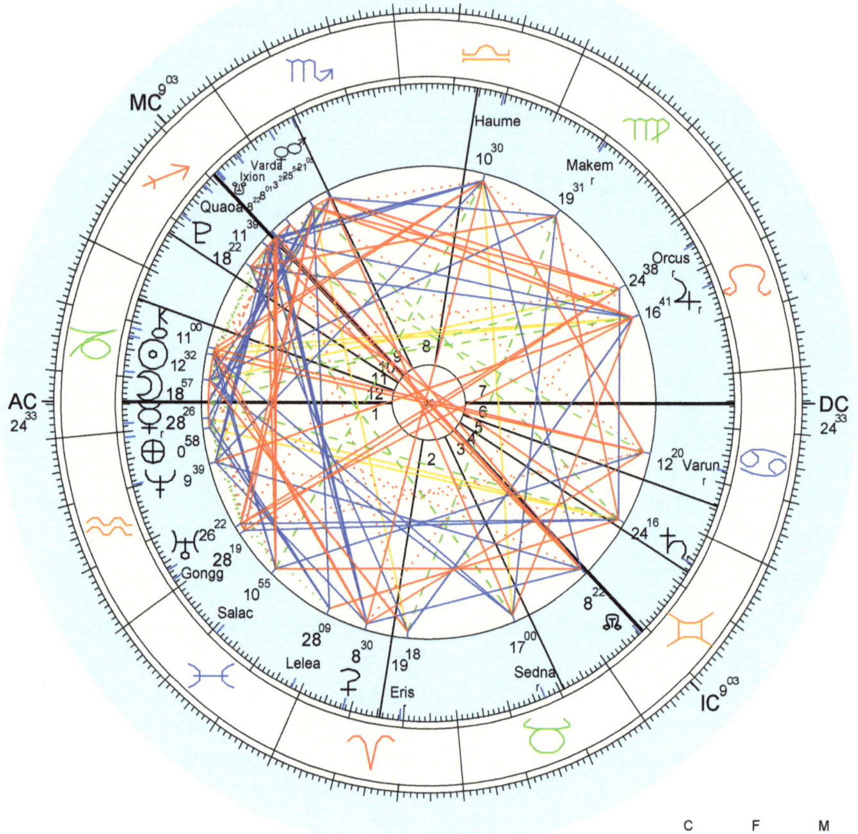

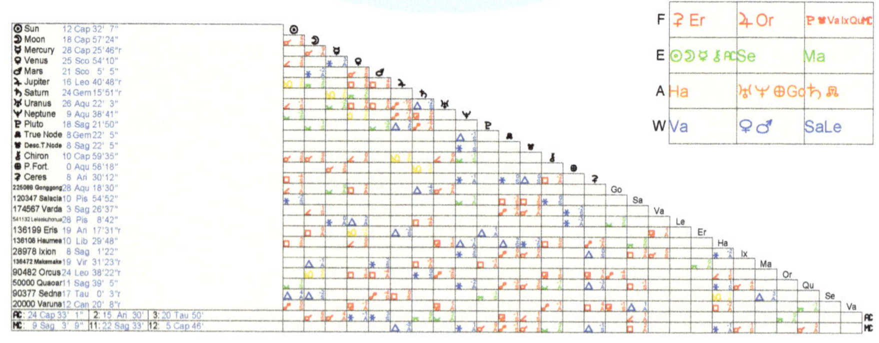

	C	F	M
F	⚳ Er	♃ Or	♇ ☋ Va Ix Qu MC
E	☉ ☽ ☿ ⚷ AC	Se	Ma
A	Ha	♅ ♆ ⊕ Go	♄ ☊
W	Va	♀ ♂	Sa Le

☉ Sun	12 Cap 32' 7"
☽ Moon	18 Cap 57'24"
☿ Mercury	28 Cap 25'46"r
♀ Venus	25 Sco 54'10"
♂ Mars	21 Sco 5' 5"
♃ Jupiter	16 Leo 40'48"r
♄ Saturn	24 Gem 15'51"r
♅ Uranus	26 Aqu 22' 3"
♆ Neptune	9 Aqu 38'41"
♇ Pluto	18 Sag 21'50"
☊ True Node	8 Gem 22' 5"
☋ Desc.T.Node	8 Sag 22' 5"
⚷ Chiron	10 Cap 59'35"
⊕ P.Fort.	0 Aqu 58'18"
⚳ Ceres	8 Ari 30'12"
225088 Gonggong	28 Aqu 18'30"
120347 Salacia	10 Pis 54'52"
174567 Varda	3 Sag 26'37"
541132 Leleakuhonua	28 Pis 8'42"
136199 Eris	19 Ari 17'31"r
136108 Haumea	10 Lib 29'48"
28978 Ixion	8 Sag 1'22"
136472 Makemake	19 Vir 31'23"r
90482 Orcus	24 Leo 38'22"r
50000 Quaoar	11 Sag 39' 5"
90377 Sedna	17 Tau 0' 3"r
20000 Varuna	12 Can 20' 8"r

AC: 24 Cap 33' 1"	2: 15 Ari 30'	3: 20 Tau 50'
MC: 9 Sag 3' 9"	11: 22 Sag 33'	12: 5 Cap 46'

issue that everyone is responsible for addressing, and her interactions connect the abstract science to each of our personal futures, showing that all our actions have consequences for generations to come.

Started School Strike

So let's have a look at her transits on the day she started her strike, the 20th August 2018. That day she had transiting Ixion opposite her Saturn and semi-square her Neptune, as she spoke her authentic truth to power, sitting alone with her sign outside the Swedish parliament.

Fortunately, transiting Uranus was closely biquintile her natal Ixion, and transiting Ixion was closely sextile her natal Uranus, enabling her message to spread through the media and online networks. She gained significant media attention within days, which inspired other students to join her. The movement grew from a solo protest to a global phenomenon within months, with over 17,000 students in 24 countries striking by November 2018.

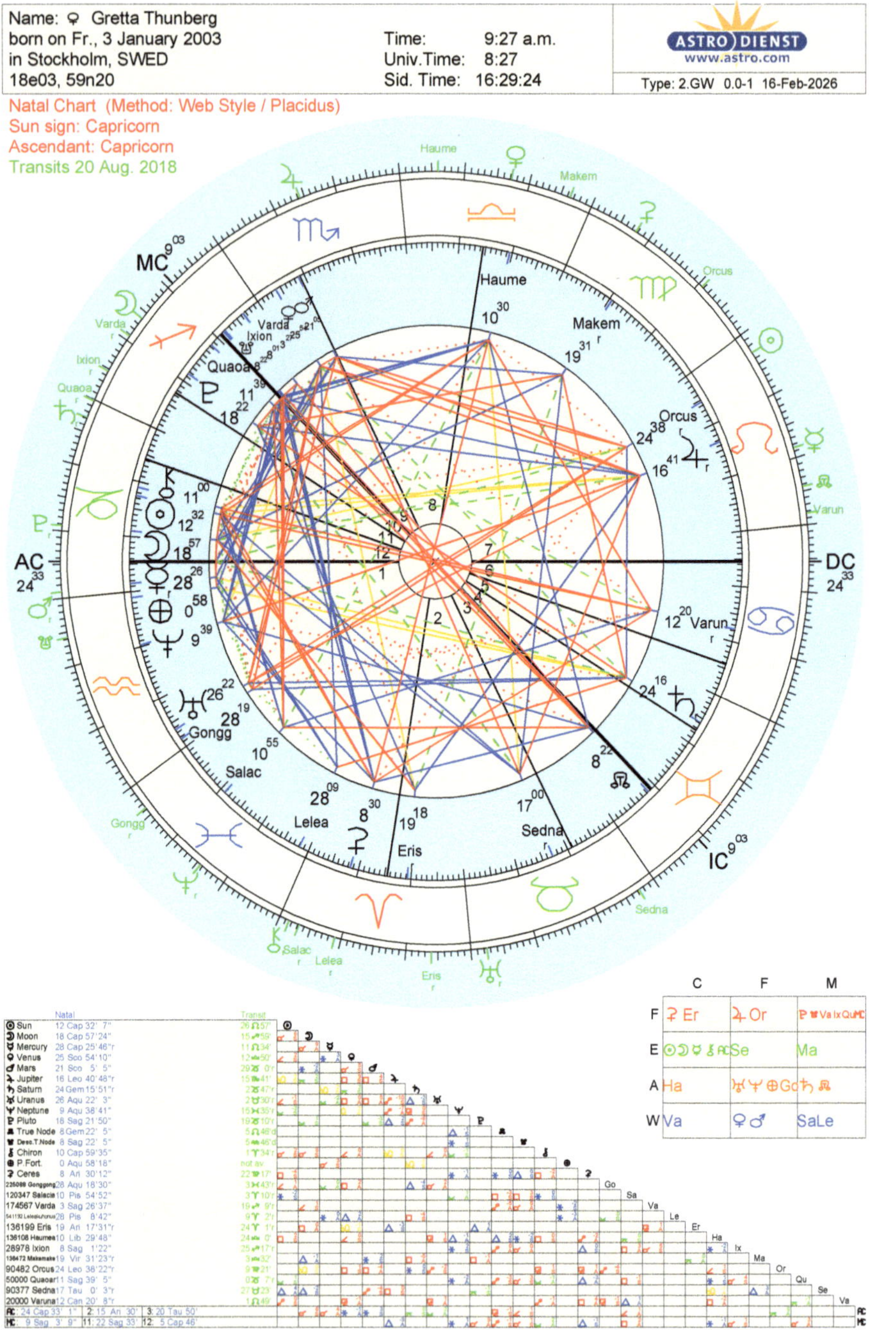

Name: ♀ Gretta Thunberg born on Fr., 3 January 2003 in Stockholm, SWED 18e03, 59n20	Time: 9:27 a.m. Univ.Time: 8:27 Sid. Time: 16:29:24	 Type: 2.GW 0.0-1 16-Feb-2026

Natal Chart (Method: Web Style / Placidus)
Sun sign: Capricorn
Ascendant: Capricorn
Transits 20 Aug. 2018

	Natal	Transit
☉ Sun	12 Cap 32' 7"	26 ♌ 57'
☽ Moon	18 Cap 57'24"	15 ♐ 59'
☿ Mercury	28 Cap 25'46"r	11 ♌ 34'
♀ Venus	25 Sco 54'10"	12 ♎ 50'
♂ Mars	21 Sco 5' 5"	29 ♑ 0'r
♃ Jupiter	16 Leo 40'48"r	15 ♏ 41'
♄ Saturn	24 Gem 15'51"r	2 ♑ 47'r
♅ Uranus	26 Aqu 22' 3"	2 ♉ 30'r
♆ Neptune	9 Aqu 38'41"	15 ♓ 35'r
♇ Pluto	18 Sag 21'50"	19 ♑ 10'r
☊ True Node	8 Gem 22' 5"	5 ♌ 46'd
☋ Desc.T.Node	8 Sag 22' 5"	5 ♒ 46'd
⚷ Chiron	10 Cap 59'35"	1 ♈ 34'r
⊕ P.Fort.	0 Aqu 58'18"	not av.
⚳ Ceres	8 Ari 30'12"	22 ♍ 17'
225088 Gonggong	28 Aqu 18'30"	3 ♓ 43'r
120347 Salacia	10 Pis 54'52"	3 ♈ 10'r
174567 Varda	3 Sag 26'37"	19 ♐ 9'r
541132 Leleakuhonua	28 Pis 8'42"	9 ♈ 2'r
136199 Eris	19 Ari 17'31"r	24 ♈ 1'r
136108 Haumea	10 Lib 29'48"	24 ♎ 0'
28978 Ixion	8 Sag 1'22"	25 ♐ 17'r
136472 Makemake	19 Vir 31'23"r	3 ♎ 32'
90482 Orcus	24 Leo 38'22"r	9 ♍ 21'
50000 Quaoar	11 Sag 39' 5"	0 ♑ 7'r
90377 Sedna	17 Tau 0' 3"r	27 ♉ 23'
20000 Varuna	12 Can 20' 8"r	1 ♌ 49'

AC: 24 Cap 33' 1"	2: 15 Ari 30'	3: 20 Tau 50'
MC: 9 Sag 3' 9"	11: 22 Sag 33'	12: 5 Cap 46'

	C	F	M
F	⚳ Er	♃ Or	♇ ☋ Va Ix Qu MC
E	☉ ☽ ☿ ⚷ AC	Se	Ma
A	Ha	♅ ♆ ⊕ Go	♄ ☊
W	Va	♀ ♂	Sa Le

Global School Climate Strike

Together, they organised a school climate strike movement and a global strike on 15 March 2019 gathered more than one million strikers. On this date she had transiting Pluto closely semi-square her natal Ixion as her authenticity faced up to power.

Name: ♀ Gretta Thunberg	Time: 9:27 a.m.
born on Fr., 3 January 2003	Univ.Time: 8:27
in Stockholm, SWED	Sid. Time: 16:29:24
18e03, 59n20	

Type: 2.GW 0.0-1 16-Feb-2026

Natal Chart (Method: Web Style / Placidus)
Sun sign: Capricorn
Ascendant: Capricorn
Transits 15 Mar. 2019

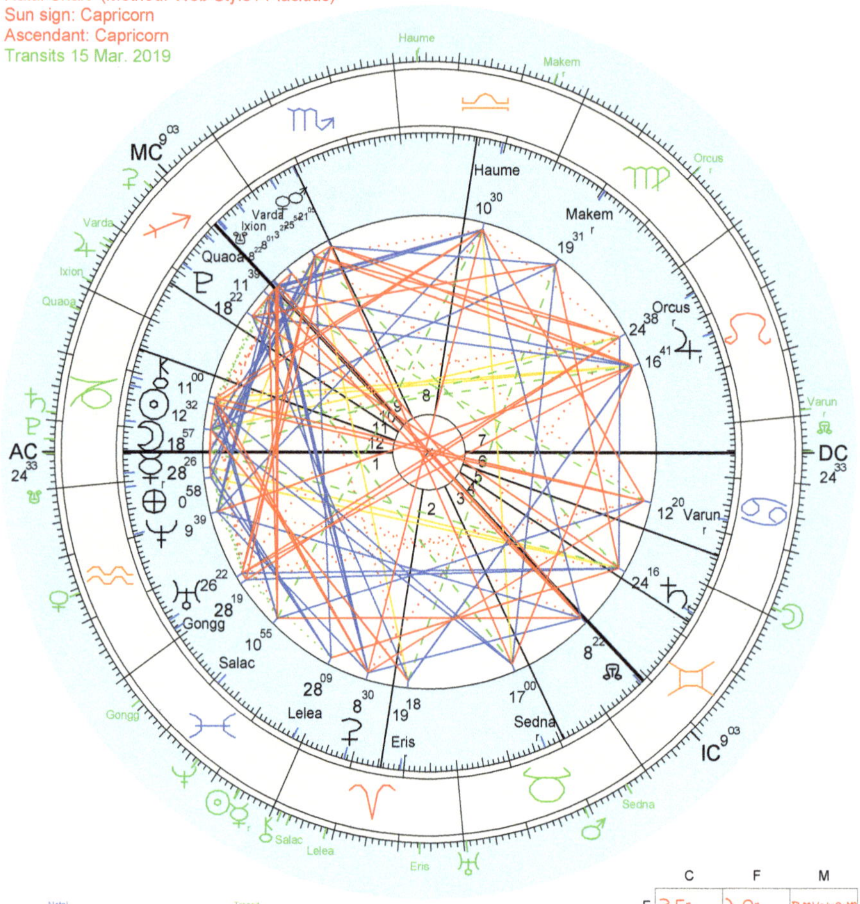

	Natal	Transit
☉ Sun	12 Cap 32' 7"	24 ♓ 7'
☽ Moon	18 Cap 57'24"	1 ♊ 15'
☿ Mercury	28 Cap 25'46"r	24 ♓ 16'r
♀ Venus	25 Sco 54'10"	15 ♒ 50'
♂ Mars	21 Sco 5' 5"	19 ♉ 11'
♃ Jupiter	16 Leo 40'48"r	23 ♐ 15'
♄ Saturn	24 Gem 15'51"r	18 ♑ 50'
♅ Uranus	26 Aqu 22' 3"	0 ♉ 24'
♆ Neptune	9 Aqu 38'41"	16 ♓ 28'
♇ Pluto	18 Sag 21'50"	22 ♑ 45'
☊ True Node	8 Gem 22' 5"	24 ♋ 50'd
☋ Desc.T.Node	8 Sag 22' 5"	24 ♑ 50'd
⚷ Chiron	10 Cap 58'35"	1 ♈ 23'
⊕ P.Fort	0 Aqu 58'18"	not av
⚳ Ceres	8 Ari 30'12"	12 ♐ 18'
225088 Gonggong	28 Aqu 18'30"	4 ♓ 1'
120347 Salacia	10 Pis 54'52"	2 ♈ 49'
174567 Varda	3 Sag 26'37"	22 ♐ 22'
541132 Leleakuhonua	28 Pis 8'42"	8 ♈ 43'
136199 Eris	19 Ari 17'31"r	23 ♈ 20'
136108 Haumea	10 Lib 29'48"	26 ♎ 23'r
28978 Ixion	8 Sag 1'22"	28 ♐ 48'
136472 Makemake	19 Vir 31'23"r	5 ♎ 5'r
90482 Orcus	24 Leo 38'22"r	9 ♍ 55'r
50000 Quaoar	11 Sag 39' 5"	3 ♑ 19'
90377 Sedna	17 Tau 0' 3"r	26 ♉ 26'
20000 Varuna	12 Can 20' 8"r	0 ♌ 53'r

AC: 24 Cap 33' 1"	2: 15 Ari 30'	3: 20 Tau 50'
MC: 9 Sag 3' 9"	11: 22 Sag 33'	12: 5 Cap 46'

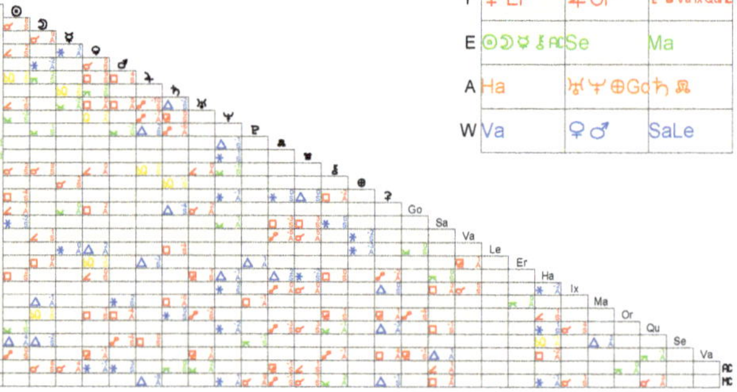

	C	F	M
F	⚳ Er	♃ Or	♇ ☋ Va Ix Qu MC
E	☉ ☽ ☿ ⚷ AC	Se	Ma
A	Ha	♅ ♆ ⊕ Go	♄ ☊
W	Va	♀ ♂	SaLe

And transiting Eris, our new planet of diversity consciousness, was sesquiquadrate her Ixion. Eris is the higher octave of Pluto, lifting his transformative energy into a fierce grace and giving us a female power that is initially gentle in its contact, but rises to meet the needs of any occasion. Eris is a truth-teller, and she can give us an inner wisdom, or a connection with a spirit guide, so the sesquiquadrate was challenging Gretta to authentically express her truth and embrace her female power.

At the same time, transiting Ixion was still sextile her Uranus within 2 degrees, as she fostered the activist network that she had built over the past year. And it was now closely semi-sextile her Mercury, as they collectively delivered her message of the need for change.

Transiting Ixion was also closely sextile her natal Gonggong, our new planet of empathic consciousness. Gonggong is the higher octave of Salacia, lifting her psychic one-to-one contact into an ability to channel group psychic and emotional energies and thereby motivate people from the inside. So, this transit gave her the ability to channel the collective energies and raise the spiritual frequency of those involved in the strike and those who heard about it.

And finally, transiting Ixion was also closely quintile her natal Salacia, our new planet of higher love consciousness. We've seen how her natal square to Salacia enables her to mix wit, memes, and selfdeprecating bio edits to keep her activism light and accessible, while still delivering pointed messages. Under the transiting quintile, the success of the Global School Climate Strike was due to her developing authenticity combining at a deep level with her natal ability to appeal to people in a way they can relate to.

UN Climate Action Speech

Gretta gave a powerful speech to the UN Climate Action Summit on the 23rd September 2019, when her transiting North Node was closely biquintile her Ixion, showing the destined nature of the opportunity it gave her to say that "the rules we're playing by are not the right ones".

At the time transiting Eris was still closely sesquiquadrate her Ixion, showing the longer phasal nature of the outer planet transits, as she rose to the challenge to authentically express her higher wisdom and embrace her female power. The speech's raw emotion and direct criticism of world leaders solidified her as a central figure in the youth climate movement and a major voice for climate justice.

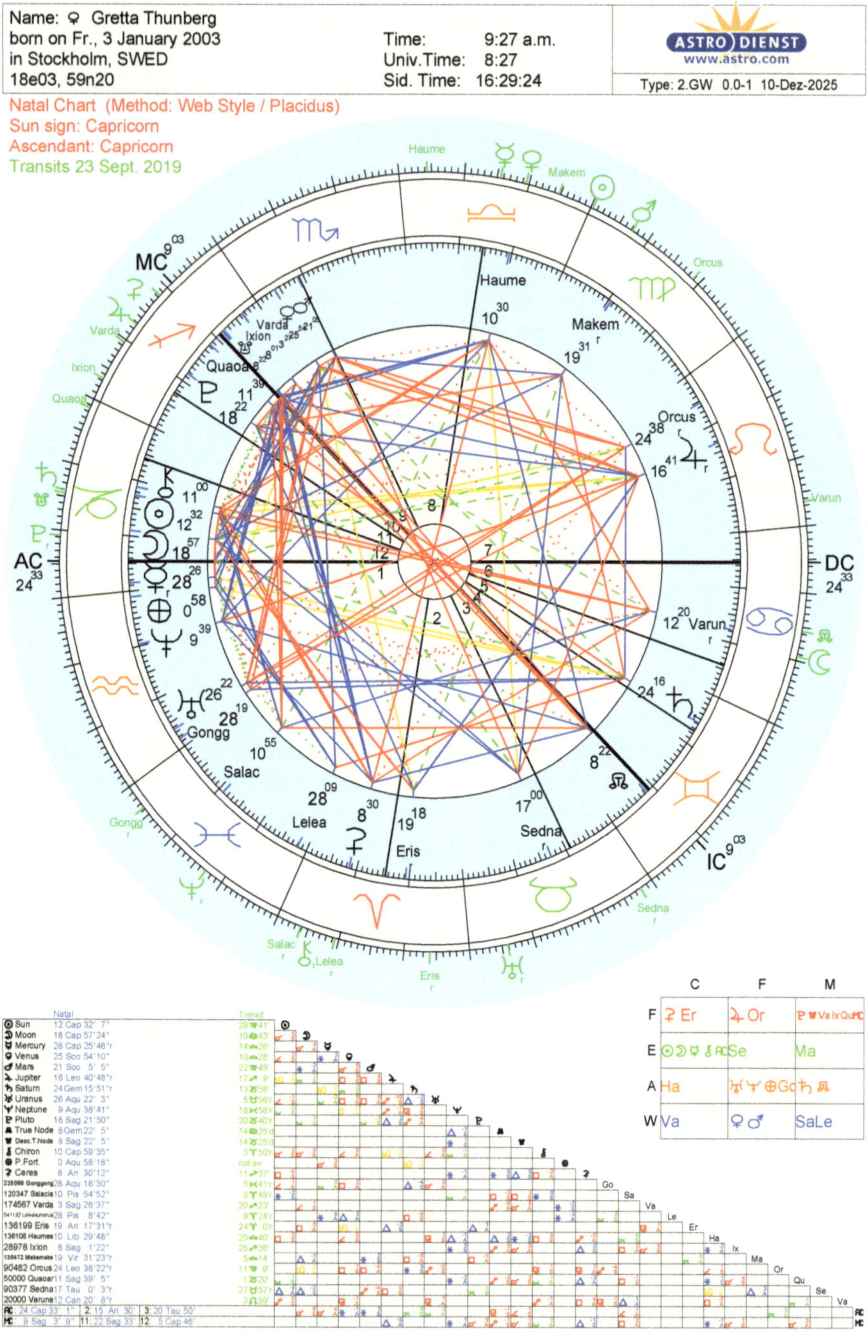

Name: ♀ Gretta Thunberg
born on Fr., 3 January 2003 Time: 9:27 a.m.
in Stockholm, SWED Univ.Time: 8:27
18e03, 59n20 Sid. Time: 16:29:24

Type: 2.GW 0.0-1 10-Dez-2025

Natal Chart (Method: Web Style / Placidus)
Sun sign: Capricorn
Ascendant: Capricorn
Transits 23 Sept. 2019

	Natal	Transit
☉ Sun	12 Cap 32' 7"	29 ♍ 41'
☽ Moon	18 Cap 57'24"	10 ♋ 43'
☿ Mercury	28 Cap 25'46"r	14 ♎ 26'
♀ Venus	25 Sco 54'10"	10 ♎ 28'
♂ Mars	21 Sco 5' 5"	22 ♍ 49'
♃ Jupiter	16 Leo 40'48"r	17 ♐ 9'
♄ Saturn	24 Gem 15'51"r	13 ♑ 56'
♅ Uranus	26 Aqu 22' 3"	5 ♉ 56'r
♆ Neptune	9 Aqu 38'41"	16 ♓ 58'r
♇ Pluto	18 Sag 21'50"	20 ♑ 40'r
☊ True Node	8 Gem 22' 5"	14 ♋ 25'd
☋ Desc.T.Node	8 Sag 22' 5"	14 ♑ 25'd
⚷ Chiron	10 Cap 59'35"	3 ♈ 50'r
⊕ P.Fort.	0 Aqu 58'18"	not av
⚳ Ceres	8 Ari 30'12"	11 ♐ 37'
225088 Gonggong	28 Aqu 18'30"	3 ♓ 41'r
120347 Salacia	10 Pis 54'52"	3 ♈ 49'r
174567 Varda	3 Sag 26'37"	20 ♐ 23'
541132 Leleakuhonua	28 Pis 8'42"	9 ♈ 24'r
136199 Eris	19 Ari 17'31"r	24 ♈ 0'r
136108 Haumea	10 Lib 29'48"	25 ♎ 40'
28978 Ixion	8 Sag 1'22"	26 ♐ 36'
136472 Makemake	19 Vir 31'23"r	5 ♎ 14'
90482 Orcus	24 Leo 38'22"r	11 ♍ 9'
50000 Quaoar	11 Sag 39' 5"	1 ♑ 20'
90377 Sedna	17 Tau 0' 3"r	27 ♉ 57'r
20000 Varuna	12 Can 20' 8"r	3 ♌ 39'

AC: 24 Cap 33' 1"	2: 15 Ari 30'	3: 20 Tau 50'
MC: 9 Sag 3' 9"	11: 22 Sag 33'	12: 5 Cap 46'

	C	F	M
F	⚳ Er	♃ Or	♇ ☋ Va Ix Qu MC
E	☉ ☽ ☿ ⚷ AC Se		Ma
A	Ha	♅ ♆ ⊕ Go	♄ ☊
W	Va	♀ ♂	Sa Le

On that day transiting Ixion was semi-sextile her Venus, and again closely sextile her Uranus, as her activism fostered her relationships and her network. Her speech created massive global media attention, mobilizing more activists to join her cause, and drawing the attention of influential figures and organizations.

Case Study – Alan Clay

I'm going to use myself as a case study, because I have Ixion sitting in my 10th House in Libra and many of you will know that I worked extensively earlier in my life as a clown and a clown teacher. I'm just going to explode the stereotypes to start with here to state that clown is an emotional art form which works on a psychic level to release blocks and tension in the audience. It is a very hard thing to teach because there are no rules, essentially it is a lawless art form.

For quite a while I've been thankful of finding the clown work in my early 20s, particularly when I looked at my 10th House Ixion placement, because clown is probably one of the best ways to be lawless in society. I also have a Sun Saturn conjunction in Scorpio in the 11th House, which is a bit of a judgemental combination that can stifle action through fear, particularly when it is square Mars in Aquarius in the 2nd.

In clown I found a great freedom from judgement, because mistakes are treasures to be explored, and there is no such thing as failure. And I found that freedom when I went to a Fools School in Stockholm, Sweden, as transiting Ixion first conjuncted my Saturn.

While we have an understanding of clown that comes largely from the circus, the fool is a more archetypal figure. The fool in the Tarot deck steps happily off a cliff but doesn't see the problem and so there isn't one. The card represents new beginnings and having faith in the future. It talks of being inexperienced and not knowing what to expect, but of having beginner's luck which comes through improvisation and by believing in the universe.

Fools School

Fools School started on 1st November 1977, when the conjunction of transiting Ixion to my natal Saturn was just coming into a 1-degree orb. The closest aspect however at that point was the square to my Mars, so the challenge for me during Fools School was to be authentic. Clown work is improvised theatre where the magic of the story is created spontaneously in the interaction in each moment.

Transiting Ixion was also closely quintile my natal Chiron in the first house. The quintiles are evolutionary opportunities that we have to practise to develop, and I look at the wounding and healing of Chiron as

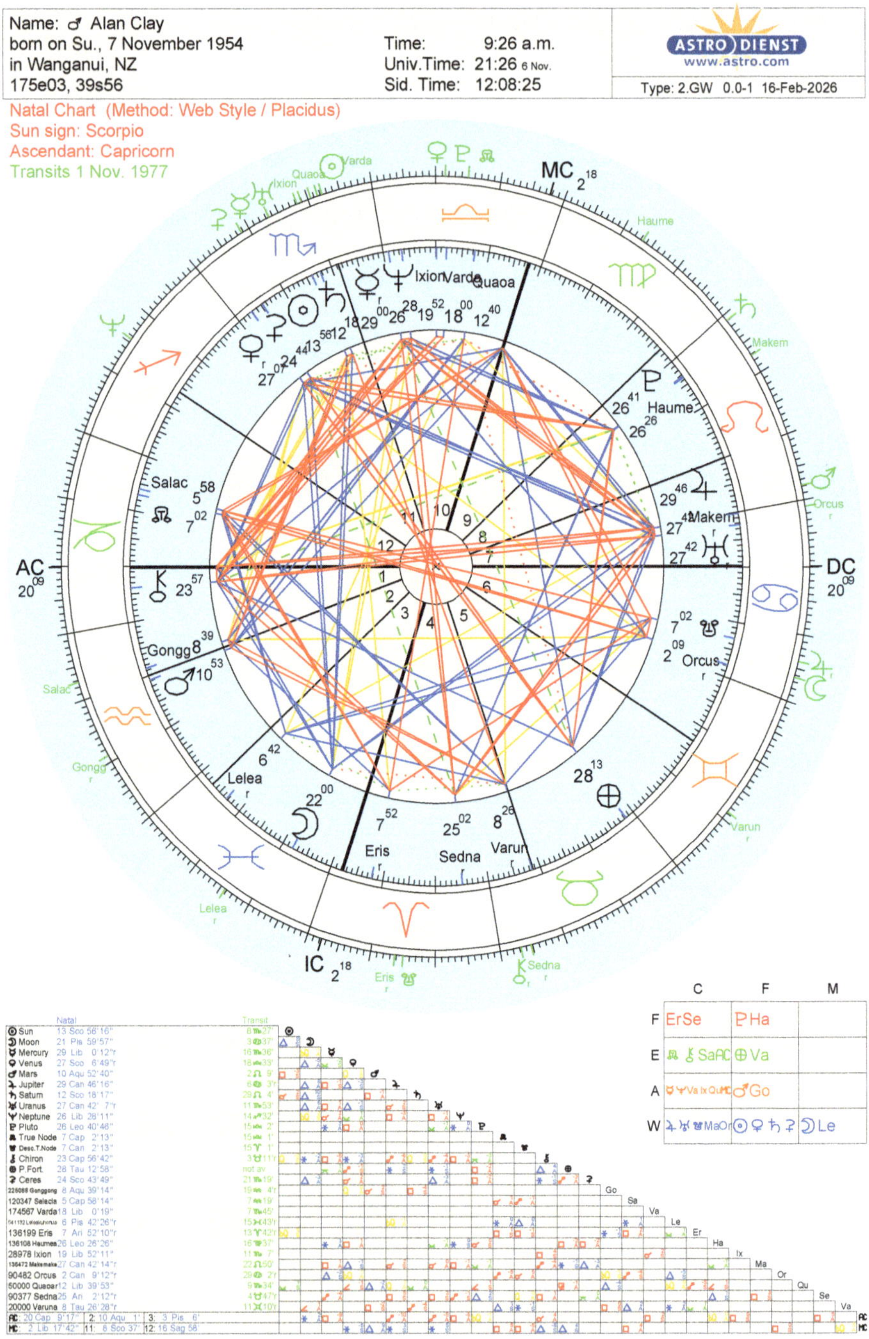

Name: ♂ Alan Clay born on Su., 7 November 1954 in Wanganui, NZ 175e03, 39s56	Time: 9:26 a.m. Univ.Time: 21:26 6 Nov. Sid. Time: 12:08:25	 Type: 2.GW 0.0-1 16-Feb-2026

Natal Chart (Method: Web Style / Placidus)
Sun sign: Scorpio
Ascendant: Capricorn
Transits 1 Nov. 1977

	Natal	Transit
☉ Sun	13 Sco 56'16"	8 ♏ 27'
☽ Moon	21 Pis 59'57"	3 ♋ 37'
☿ Mercury	29 Lib 0'12"r	16 ♏ 36'
♀ Venus	27 Sco 6'49"r	18 ♎ 33'
♂ Mars	10 Aqu 52'40"	2 ♌ 9'
♃ Jupiter	29 Can 46'16"	6 ♋ 3'r
♄ Saturn	12 Sco 18'17"	29 ♌ 4'
♅ Uranus	27 Can 42' 7"r	11 ♏ 53'
♆ Neptune	26 Lib 28'11"	14 ♐ 32'
♇ Pluto	26 Leo 40'46"	15 ♎ 2'
☊ True Node	7 Cap 2'13"	15 ♎ 1'
☋ Desc.T.Node	7 Can 2'13"	15 ♈ 1'
⚷ Chiron	23 Cap 56'42"	3 ♉ 11'r
⊕ P.Fort.	28 Tau 12'58"	not av
⚳ Ceres	24 Sco 43'49"	21 ♏ 19'
225088 Gonggong	8 Aqu 39'14"	19 ♒ 4'r
120347 Salacia	5 Cap 58'14"	7 ♒ 19'
174567 Varda	18 Lib 0'19"	7 ♏ 45'
541132 Leleakuhonua	6 Pis 42'26"r	15 ♓ 43'r
136199 Eris	7 Ari 52'10"r	13 ♈ 42'r
136108 Haumea	26 Leo 26'26"	16 ♍ 37'
28978 Ixion	19 Lib 52'11"	11 ♏ 7'
136472 Makemake	27 Can 42'14"r	22 ♌ 50'
90482 Orcus	2 Can 9'12"r	29 ♋ 2'r
50000 Quaoar	12 Lib 39'53"	9 ♏ 34'
90377 Sedna	25 Ari 2'12"r	4 ♉ 47'r
20000 Varuna	8 Tau 26'28"r	11 ♊ 10'r

AC: 20 Cap 9'17"	2: 10 Aqu 1'	3: 3 Pis 6'
MC: 2 Lib 17'42"	11: 8 Sco 37'	12: 16 Sag 58'

	C	F	M
F	ErSe	♇Ha	
E	☊ ⚷ SaAC	⊕ Va	
A	☿♆Va IxQuMC	♂Go	
W	♃♅☋MaOr	☉♀♄⚳	☽Le

a growth process. So, Fools School enabled me to grow out of the fearful judgementalness of my natal Saturn-Sun square Mars and learn to be creative in each moment.

The close transit to my natal Ixion during this time was a trine from transiting Gonggong, our new planet of empathy consciousness. Clown is an art form which connects with the audience on an emotional level and I see my attraction to it in my natal conjunction of Mars and Gonggong. In my performance work I learned to take my impulses from my interactions with members of the audience.

Gonggong can channel energies and connect with people in their inner world, so the trine from transiting Gonggong to my natal Ixion opened me to find my authenticity in that emotional work with the audience. I learned that the audience brings a rich feast of emotions to the show for us to work with, and that at the heart of that experience I am always me, so I grew to trust in that interplay.

Playspace Studio - Auckland

I worked as a street clown for the next six years as Ixion transited back and forth over my Saturn-Sun conjunction and by the last hit on my Sun, I was teaching my own clown school in Auckland, New Zealand.

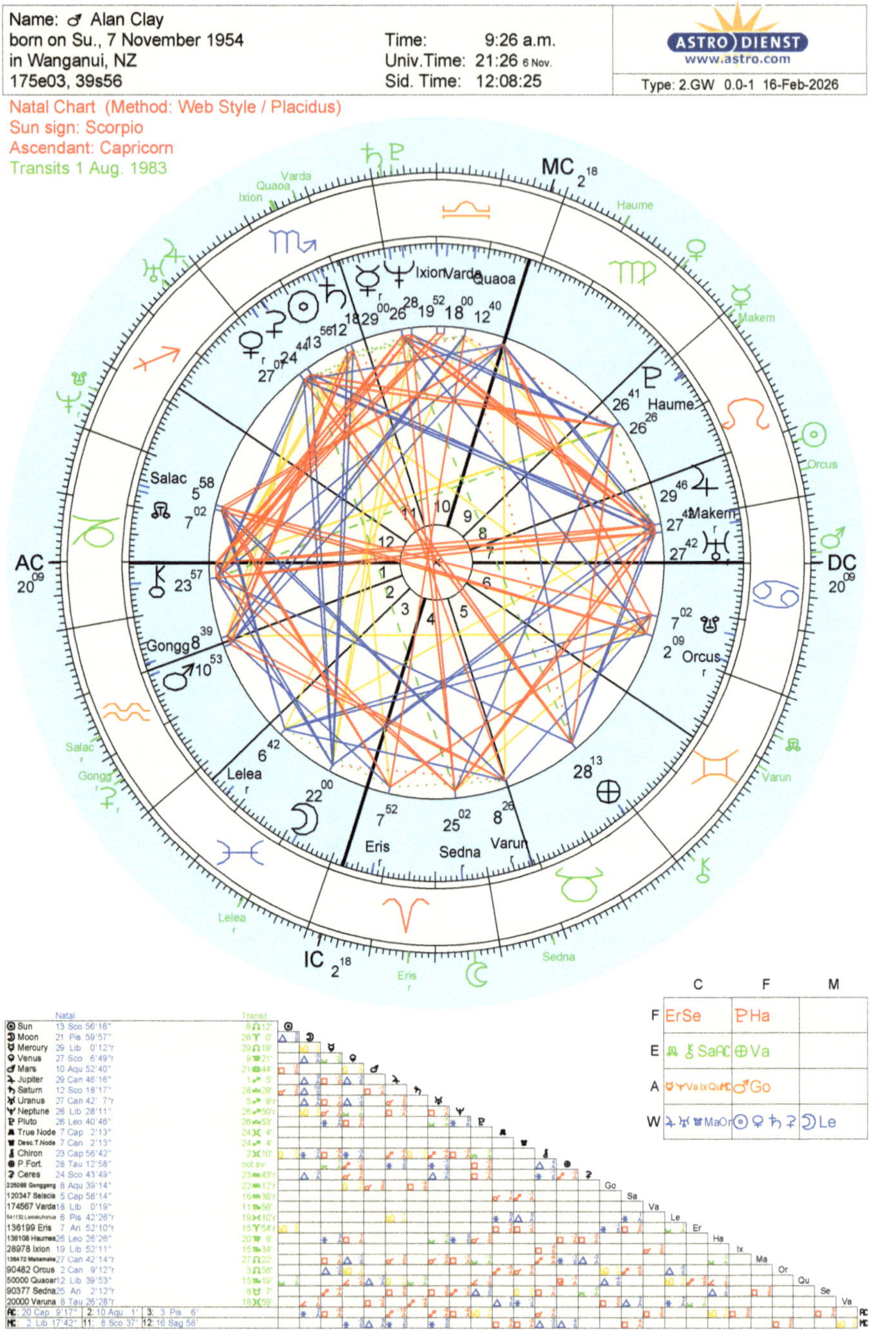

Name: ♂ Alan Clay
born on Su., 7 November 1954
in Wanganui, NZ
175e03, 39s56

Time: 9:26 a.m.
Univ.Time: 21:26 6 Nov.
Sid. Time: 12:08:25

Type: 2.GW 0.0-1 16-Feb-2026

Natal Chart (Method: Web Style / Placidus)
Sun sign: Scorpio
Ascendant: Capricorn
Transits 1 Aug. 1983

	Natal	Transit
☉ Sun	13 Sco 56'16"	8 ♌ 12'
☽ Moon	21 Pis 59'57"	26 ♈ 0'
☿ Mercury	29 Lib 0'12"r	29 ♌ 19'
♀ Venus	27 Sco 6'49"r	9 ♍ 21'
♂ Mars	10 Aqu 52'40"	21 ♋ 44'
♃ Jupiter	29 Can 46'16"	1 ♐ 5'
♄ Saturn	12 Sco 18'17"	28 ♎ 28'
♅ Uranus	27 Can 42' 7"r	5 ♐ 9'r
♆ Neptune	26 Lib 28'11"	26 ♐ 50'r
♇ Pluto	26 Leo 40'46"	26 ♎ 53'
☊ True Node	7 Cap 2'13"	24 ♊ 4'
☋ Desc.T.Node	7 Can 2'13"	24 ♐ 4'
⚷ Chiron	23 Cap 56'42"	2 ♊ 10'
⊕ P.Fort.	28 Tau 12'58"	not av
⚳ Ceres	24 Sco 43'49"	23 ♒ 43'r
225088 Gonggong	8 Aqu 39'14"	22 ♒ 12'r
120347 Salacia	5 Cap 58'14"	16 ♒ 38'r
174567 Varda	18 Lib 0'19"	11 ♏ 56'
541132 Leleakuhonua	6 Pis 42'26"r	19 ♓ 10'r
136199 Eris	7 Ari 52'10"r	15 ♈ 54'r
136108 Haumea	26 Leo 26'26"	20 ♍ 6'
28978 Ixion	19 Lib 52'11"	15 ♏ 34'
136472 Makemake	27 Can 42'14"r	27 ♌ 22'
90482 Orcus	2 Can 9'12"r	3 ♌ 58'
50000 Quaoar	12 Lib 39'53"	15 ♏ 19'
90377 Sedna	25 Ari 2'12"r	8 ♉ 7'
20000 Varuna	8 Tau 26'28"r	18 ♊ 59'

AC: 20 Cap 9'17"	2: 10 Aqu 1'	3: 3 Pis 6'
MC: 2 Lib 17'42"	11: 8 Sco 37'	12: 16 Sag 58'

	C	F	M
F	ErSe	♇Ha	
E	☊ ⚷ SaAC	⊕Va	
A	☿♆VaIxQuMC	♂Go	
W	♃♅☋MaOr	☉♀♄⚳	☽Le

The school started on the 1st of August 1983, and on that day the Sun was closely quintile my natal Ixion. This is an evolutionary flow bringing together my will and my seeker consciousness, enabling me to pull together all of my work with clown since the start of Fools School.

Uranus was also closely semi-square my natal Ixion, challenging me to be intuitive and authentic in my teaching. In the work at Playspace we regularly took exercises from the studio out into the street to test them out on people.

Meanwhile transiting Haumea, our new planet of spiritual rebirth, was closely semi-sextile my natal Ixion, speaking of the rebirth of clown and of my work, that the school represented. At the studio we worked without makeup or characters to develop a modern clown approach which was in touch with the audience, rather than hidden behind a mask.

And Varuna, our new planet of mastery consciousness, was transiting through my 6th house, closely trine my natal Ixion in the 10th. Varuna is the higher octave of Saturn, lifting his permission-based authority into a natural sovereignty, so this trine was encouraging me to claim my sovereignty as a teacher. Sovereignty is a dance we do with the collective psyche, where we have to claim it and at the same time others have to give it to us. And, over time through this dance, we build a following for our work.

Name: ♂ Alan Clay born on Su., 7 November 1954 in Wanganui, NZ 175e03, 39s56	Time: 9:26 a.m. Univ.Time: 21:26 6 Nov. Sid. Time: 12:08:25	 Type: 2.GW 0.0-1 17-Feb-2026

Natal Chart (Method: Web Style / Placidus)
Sun sign: Scorpio
Ascendant: Capricorn
Transits 21 Jan. 1994

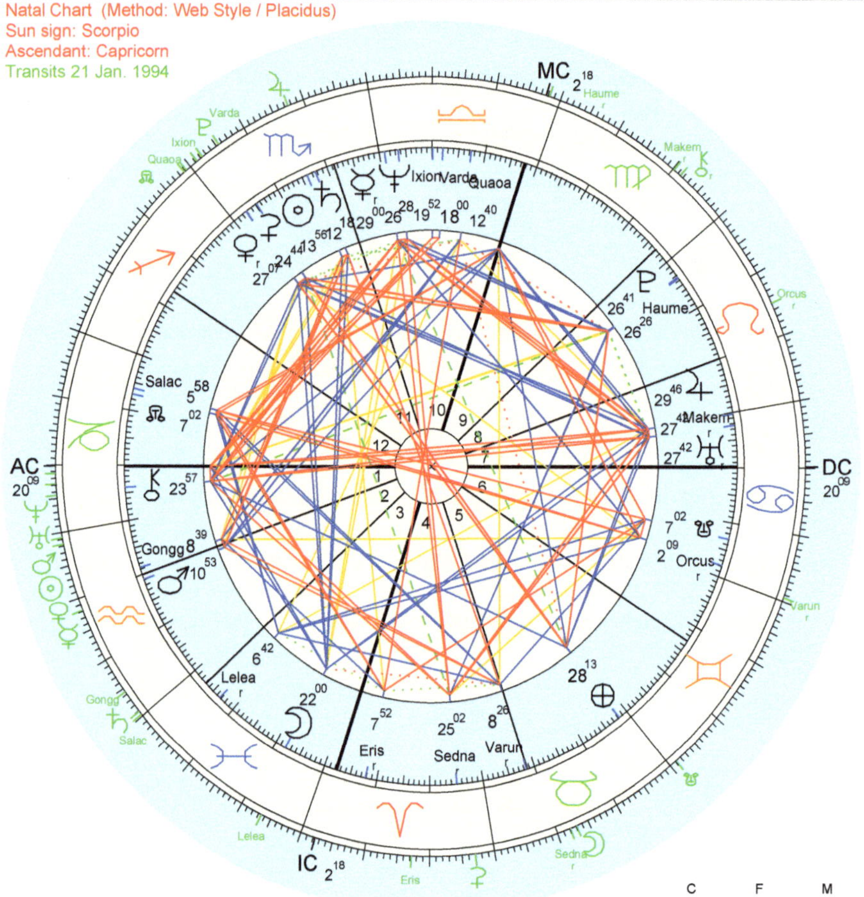

	Natal	Transit
☉ Sun	13 Sco 56'16"	0 ♒ 43'
☽ Moon	21 Pis 59'57"	13 ♉ 10'
☿ Mercury	29 Lib 0'12"r	11 ♒ 50'
♀ Venus	27 Sco 6'49"r	1 ♒ 39'
♂ Mars	10 Aqu 52'40"	24 ♑ 26'
♃ Jupiter	29 Can 46'16"	12 ♏ 26'
♄ Saturn	12 Sco 18'17"	29 ♒ 5'
♅ Uranus	27 Can 42' 7"r	22 ♑ 46'
♆ Neptune	26 Lib 28'11"	21 ♑ 13'
♇ Pluto	26 Leo 40'46"	27 ♏ 37'
☊ True Node	7 Cap 2'13"	1 ♐ 10'd
☋ Desc.T.Node	7 Can 2'13"	1 ♊ 10'd
⚷ Chiron	23 Cap 56'42"	8 ♍ 33'r
⊕ P.Fort.	28 Tau 12'58"	not av
⚳ Ceres	24 Sco 43'49"	27 ♈ 4'
225088 Gonggong	8 Aqu 39'14"	25 ♒ 30'
120347 Salacia	5 Cap 58'14"	29 ♒ 38'
174567 Varda	18 Lib 0'19"	24 ♏ 28'
541132 Leleakuhonua	6 Pis 42'26"r	23 ♓ 24'
136199 Eris	7 Ari 52'10"r	17 ♈ 13'
136108 Haumea	26 Leo 26'26"	1 ♎ 44'r
28978 Ixion	19 Lib 52'11"	28 ♏ 39'
136472 Makemake	27 Can 42'14"r	9 ♍ 48'r
90482 Orcus	2 Can 9'12"r	15 ♌ 2'r
50000 Quaoar	12 Lib 39'53"	0 ♐ 47'
90377 Sedna	25 Ari 2'12"r	12 ♉ 7'r
20000 Varuna	8 Tau 26'28"r	0 ♋ 37'r

AC: 20 Cap 9'17"	2: 10 Aqu 1'	3: 3 Pis 6'
MC: 2 Lib 17'42"	11: 8 Sco 37'	12: 16 Sag 58'

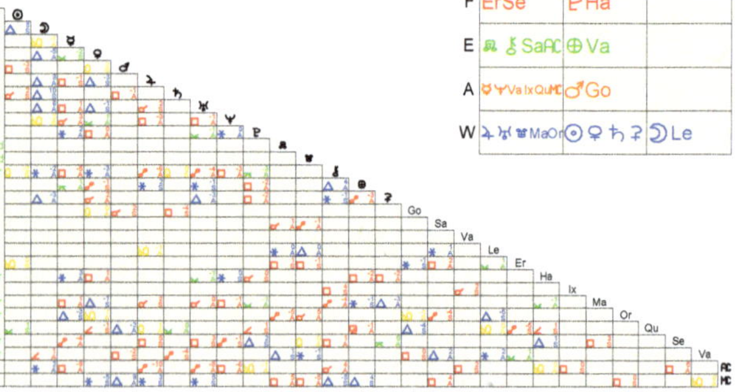

	C	F	M
F	ErSe	♇Ha	
E	☊ ⚷ SaAC	⊕ Va	
A	☿♆VaIxQuMC	♂Go	
W	♃♅☋MaOr	☉♀♄⚳	☽Le

Moontan

I worked on my first novel about a clown called Moontan for some years, and I have natal Venus in Scorpio in the 11th House, square Pluto in Leo in the 8th. As Ixion came up to conjunct my Venus, I spent some time submitting the manuscript to publishers and getting rejected. Until finally, a New Zealand publisher got a good reader's report, and I flew over from Australia.

Publishers don't read new manuscripts themselves they hire readers they trust to do that. So, I was thrilled to hear that he had got a good report, and I turned up at the meeting to be told that, *"This is not your first book."* *"Yes,"* I protested, *"it is my first book."* I knew I hadn't written one before. *"No," he repeated "this is not your first."*

Apparently while the first reader's report had sung the praises of my book, he had sent out for a second report to be on the safe side, and the second had said *'Don't take this one, encourage him to write another and look at that'.*

Fortunately, Short Run Printing had just come in, meaning I could print just a thousand books and still make a profit selling them at market rates. This was the forerunner of today's Print on Demand. So as transiting Ixion was conjunct my natal Venus, meaning that my developing authenticity was together with my values and relationships, I submitted the files to self-publish the book.

Transiting Ixion was also closely quintile my Mars that day, giving me an evolutionary opportunity to take action. And it was trine my Jupiter, Uranus, Makemake conjunction in the 7th house. Makemake is our new planet of systems consciousness, which enables us to build a model of the world, and of our place in that reality, through the experiences that we have in our lives. I see this conjunction as my clown adventure point, where I go out into the world and interact with people in an improvised way and learn from that experience.

Playspace Studio - Sydney

I re-established Playspace Studio, a circus and physical theatre studio, in Sydney, Australia, in the late 90s. As I rented the studio, on the 28th February 1998, transiting Ixion was closely sextile my MC, talking about the social platform I was creating which would enable my independent teaching work.

Transiting Ixion was also closely semi-square my natal Varda, our new planet of inspiration consciousness, which I have conjunct my natal Ixion in my 10th house. Varda is the Elven goddess from the mythology of *The Lord of the Rings*, who enables us to win our battles with the dark forces in our lives through hope and inspiration and who can lead us through a transition to a new state of being.

That is a pretty good description of what happens in a clown performance or in a clown workshop. So, the semi-square from transiting Ixion to Varda is saying that the work at the studio would be hope-filled and light-filled, and able to help students through a transition to a new state of being - as a clown.

And, at the same time, transiting Jupiter was closely conjunct transiting Salacia, our new planet of higher love consciousness, with both closely sesquiquadrate my natal Ixion. The Jupiter sesquiquadrate is talking about the opportunity for expansion that the studio would provide. And the Salacia sesquiquadrate is saying that the work at the studio would be intimate, light-hearted and process-based, and that it would be appealing even if it is confronting. We saw in the previous case study on Gretta Thunberg how Salacia brings a lightness of heart and a psychic intimacy which enables our message to connect with more people, so the semi-square is also saying that the work at the studio will be popular.

Meanwhile transiting Saturn and transiting Eris, our new planet of diversity consciousness, were closely conjunct in my 4th house, with both opposite my natal Ixion within 2 degrees. The Saturn opposition is talking about how the studio will provide a structure for my independent seeker consciousness to interact with society. And Eris is saying that it will be a sacred space in which there will be no judgement or comparison and everyone will be valued for who they are.

Undercover Clown

Melkweg Multimedia Centre,
Amsterdam, 1985

Name: ♂ Alan Clay		
born on Su., 7 November 1954	Time: 9:26 a.m.	
in Wanganui, NZ	Univ.Time: 21:26 6 Nov.	
175e03, 39s56	Sid. Time: 12:08:25	Type: 2.GW 0.0-1 17-Feb-2026

Transits 28 Feb. 1998

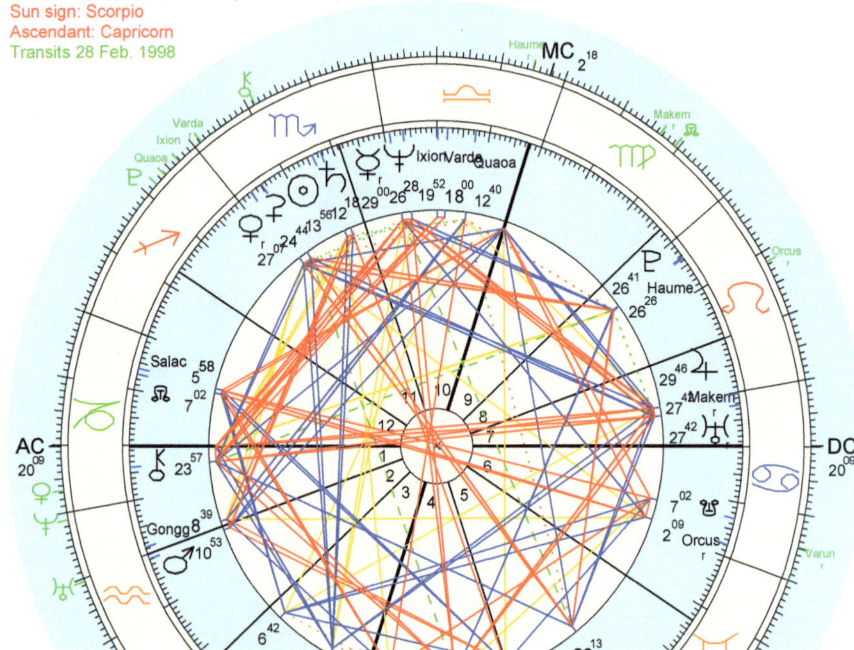

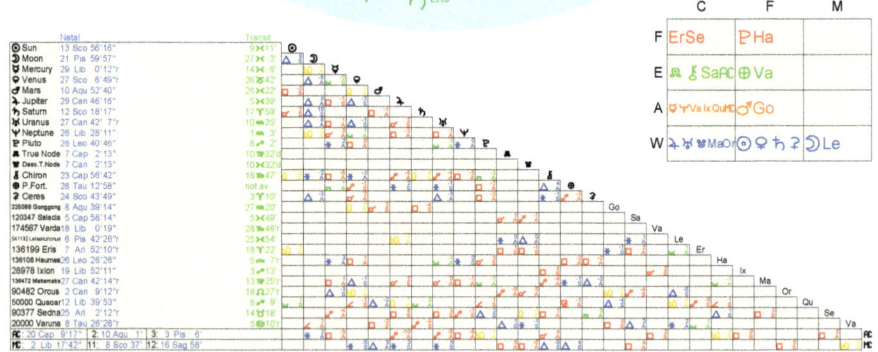

	Natal	Transit
☉ Sun	13 Sco 56'16"	9 ♓ 11'
☽ Moon	21 Pis 59'57"	27 ♓ 3'
☿ Mercury	29 Lib 0'12"r	14 ♓ 6'
♀ Venus	27 Sco 6'49"r	26 ♑ 42'
♂ Mars	10 Aqu 52'40"	26 ♓ 22'
♃ Jupiter	29 Can 46'16"	5 ♓ 39'
♄ Saturn	12 Sco 18'17"	17 ♈ 59'
♅ Uranus	27 Can 42' 7"r	10 ♒ 25'
♆ Neptune	26 Lib 28'11"	1 ♒ 3'
♇ Pluto	26 Leo 40'46"	8 ♐ 2'
☊ True Node	7 Cap 2'13"	10 ♍ 32'd
☋ Desc.T.Node	7 Can 2'13"	10 ♓ 32'd
⚷ Chiron	23 Cap 56'42"	18 ♏ 47'
⊕ P.Fort.	28 Tau 12'58"	not av.
⚳ Ceres	24 Sco 43'49"	3 ♈ 10'
225088 Gonggong	8 Aqu 39'14"	27 ♒ 20'
120347 Salacia	5 Cap 58'14"	5 ♓ 49'
174567 Varda	18 Lib 0'19"	28 ♏ 46'r
541132 Leleakuhonua	6 Pis 42'26"r	25 ♓ 54'
136199 Eris	7 Ari 52'10"r	18 ♈ 22'
136108 Haumea	26 Leo 26'26"	5 ♏ 7'r
28978 Ixion	19 Lib 52'11"	3 ♐ 13'
136472 Makemake	27 Can 42'14"r	13 ♍ 25'r
90482 Orcus	2 Can 9'12"r	18 ♌ 27'r
50000 Quaoar	12 Lib 39'53"	6 ♐ 9'
90377 Sedna	25 Ari 2'12"r	14 ♉ 18'
20000 Varuna	8 Tau 26'28"r	5 ♋ 10'r

AC: 20 Cap 9'17"	2: 10 Aqu 1'	3: 3 Pis 6'
MC: 2 Lib 17'42"	11: 8 Sco 37'	12: 16 Sag 58'

	C	F	M
F	ErSe	♇Ha	
E	☊ ⚷SaAC	⊕Va	
A	☿♆Va Ix QuMC	♂Go	
W	♃♅☋MaOr	☉♀♄⚳	☽Le

In the following five years, as Ixion transited sextile my MC and then semi-sextile my North Node, and Eris transited opposite my natal Ixion, the studio gained an international recognition for the physical theatre training I was offering.

Angels Can Fly

In 2005 I put out a clown textbook, *Angels Can Fly, a Modern Clown User Guide.* I started writing this in the last year of Playspace and then finalised it over the next two years of teaching clown masterclasses internationally. During this period Ixion was transiting semi-sextile my natal North Node, so the writing was a destined expression of my developing seeker consciousness. And it was trine my natal Eris, connecting me with my inner wisdom as I wrote the book.

Angels Can Fly is an innovative book which includes a mix of theory on the nature of clown, anecdotes from some 20 international clowns, exercises for classes and workshops, and fictional stories following the adventures of 10 street clowns. It was launched at the Brisbane Writer's Festival on the 2nd September 2005. On that day I had the final touches of Ixion transiting semi-sextile my North Node and trine to Eris, as my developing seeker consciousness was flowing with my destiny and my inner spiritual truth.

Transiting Ixion was also closely inconjunct my natal Varuna, our new planet of the sovereignty that we gain through experience, which is conjunct my fifth house cusp. This is the house of passion and joy, and planets here can indicate an ability to teach your passion. So my natal Varuna placement talks of the vast experience of clown that I have built up through teaching my passion. And the inconjunct from transiting Ixion is saying that the publication of the book is a fated step enabling this passionate independent spiritual mission.

Amanda Burgess and Alan Clay performing as The Untouchables, Sydney, 1996

Transiting Ixion in my 11th house was also sextile my empathic natal Mars-Gonggong conjunction on the 2nd house cusp. Gonggong enables us to walk a mile in someone else's shoes and see the world through their eyes. So, as the book was published, my developing seeker consciousness was flowing with my natal empathy in my emotional work with the audience.

And finally transiting Ixion was in an approaching sesquiquadrate with my natal Sedna, and transiting Sedna was at the same time in a close inconjunct with my natal Ixion. Sedna is all about our spiritual destiny at the top level, but also about all the experiences that we have to go through to get to that spiritual destiny. So, the aspects between both show that the publication was an important part of my soul-growth. I believe that I have been working with clown for a number of lifetimes, and I have always said that I was moving on from that art-form in this lifetime. The publication of this book was part of the summation of that soul-growth work.

At the same time, transiting Jupiter was conjunct my natal Ixion, expanding the reach of my authentic self-expression; while transiting Pluto was sextile, empowering it; and transiting Saturn was in an approaching quintile, showing that the launch was a deeply important practical step in my life.

Transiting Eris was still opposite my natal Ixion, as it had been all through the Playspace Studio years, showing the longer phasal relationship of my developing inner wisdom and my innate seeker consciousness. The outer planet transits represent phases in our lives, and each of the exact hit's manifests as steps in this phasal journey.

And finally, transiting Varda, our planet of inspiration consciousness, was semi-square my natal Ixion, indicating that the book would inspire others who are on their own journeys. Years later I was contacted by clowns, thanking me for the book and saying how it enabled them to see the artform differently.

Here is a review which was published in the magazine, *Mask - the Journal of Drama Victoria,* in the Autumn/Winter edition 2009, giving an idea of the independent pattern breaking nature of the book:

Motivated by the belief that clown is an art form to be found in 'every culture on the planet' Clay has created a text that outlines the growth of the modern clown by blending practice with theory. His text is divided into 50 chapters, each beginning with an explanation of the particular theme whether this be, 'Bliss', 'Breath', 'Laughter' or 'Faith'. In fact, from a quick scan of such titles you could be forgiven for thinking that this is a self-help book - you would not be too wrong.

Alan and son Michael Clay performing as Snap and Crackle, Sydney, 1998

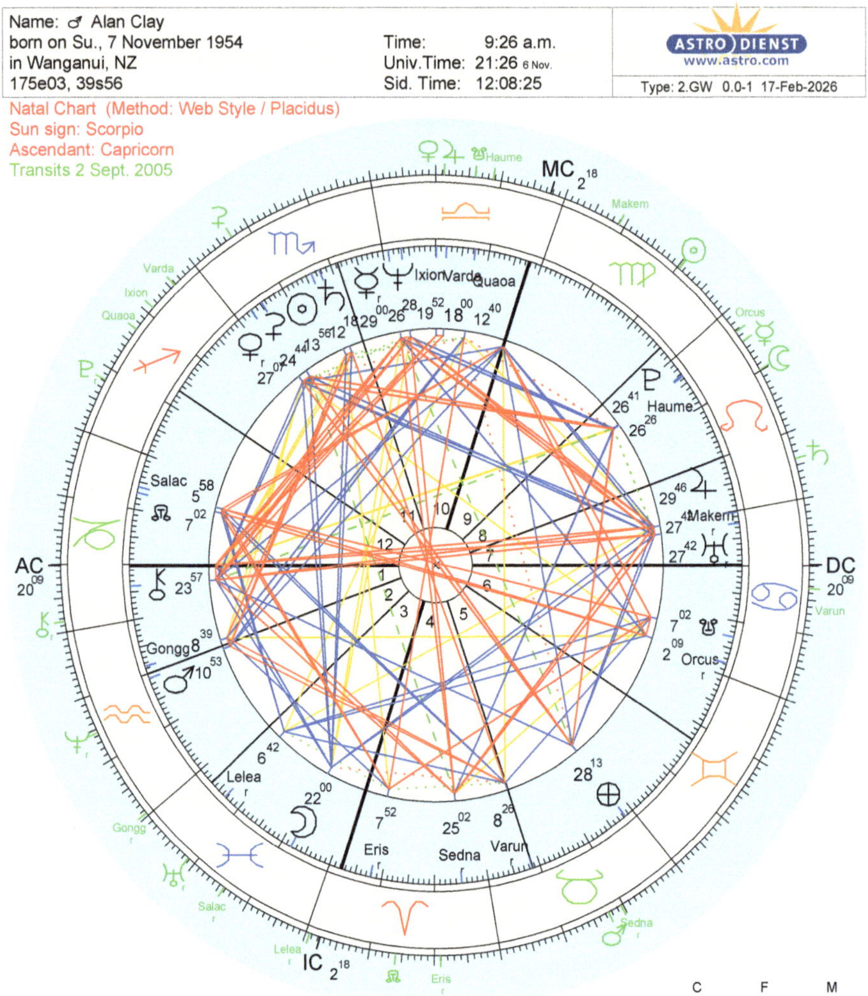

Name: ♂ Alan Clay
born on Su., 7 November 1954
in Wanganui, NZ
175e03, 39s56

Time: 9:26 a.m.
Univ.Time: 21:26 6 Nov.
Sid. Time: 12:08:25

Type: 2.GW 0.0-1 17-Feb-2026

Natal Chart (Method: Web Style / Placidus)
Sun sign: Scorpio
Ascendant: Capricorn
Transits 2 Sept. 2005

	Natal	Transit
☉ Sun	13 Sco 56'16"	9 ♍ 38'
☽ Moon	21 Pis 59'57"	20 ♌ 8'
☿ Mercury	29 Lib 0'12"r	25 ♌ 5'
♀ Venus	27 Sco 6'49"r	18 ♎ 43'
♂ Mars	10 Aqu 52'40"	17 ♉ 29'
♃ Jupiter	29 Can 46'16"	18 ♎ 42'
♄ Saturn	12 Sco 18'17"	5 ♌ 57'
♅ Uranus	27 Can 42' 7"r	8 ♓ 45'r
♆ Neptune	26 Lib 28'11"	15 ♒ 34'r
♇ Pluto	26 Leo 40'46"	21 ♐ 49'r
☊ True Node	7 Cap 2'13"	14 ♈ 1'
☋ Desc.T.Node	7 Can 2'13"	14 ♎ 1'
⚷ Chiron	23 Cap 58'42"	28 ♑ 27'r
⊕ P.Fort.	28 Tau 12'58"	not av.
⚳ Ceres	24 Sco 43'49"	22 ♏ 58'
225088 Gonggong	8 Aqu 39'14"	29 ♒ 32'r
120347 Salacia	5 Cap 58'14"	15 ♓ 44'r
174567 Varda	18 Lib 0'19"	4 ♐ 18'
541132 Leleakuhonua	6 Pis 42'26"r	0 ♈ 36'r
136199 Eris	7 Ari 52'10"r	20 ♈ 55'r
136108 Haumea	26 Leo 26'26"	11 ♎ 14'
28978 Ixion	19 Lib 52'11"	8 ♐ 59'
136472 Makemake	27 Can 42'14"r	20 ♍ 53'
90482 Orcus	2 Can 9'12"r	26 ♌ 47'
50000 Quaoar	12 Lib 39'53"	13 ♐ 3'
90377 Sedna	25 Ari 2'12"r	19 ♉ 39'r
20000 Varuna	8 Tau 26'28"r	16 ♋ 40'

AC: 20 Cap 9'17"	2: 10 Aqu 1'	3: 3 Pis 6'
MC: 2 Lib 17'42"	11: 8 Sco 37'	12: 16 Sag 58'

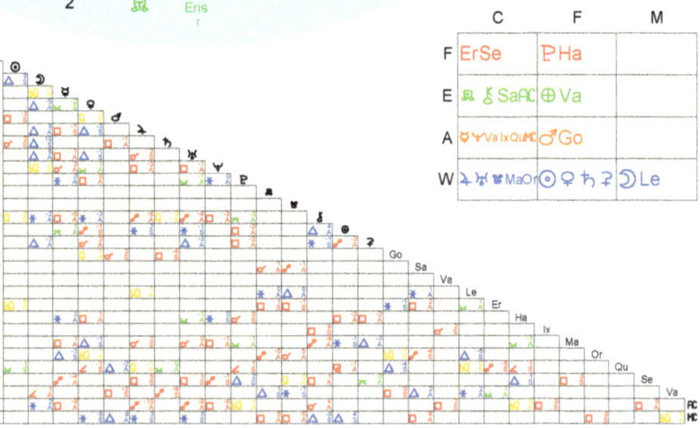

	C	F	M
F	ErSe	♇Ha	
E	☊ ⚷ SaAC	⊕ Va	
A	☿ ♆ Va Ix Qu MC	♂ Go	
W	♃ ♅ ☋ Ma Or	☉ ♀ ♄ ⚳	☽ Le

Courting Chaos

In 2012 I wrote the screenplay for a romantic comedy film, *Courting Chaos,* about a Beverly Hills girl who falls for a Venice Beach street clown called Chaos and she must overcome her inhibitions and become a clown herself for the relationship to survive.

I produced and directed this low budget film the following year, which was shot and edited at Venice Beach in Los Angeles. It was shot in a record-breaking 6 weeks from the first day of shooting, to the submission of the finished film to festivals complete with a composed soundtrack. To achieve this the editor was working on set as we shot and sending draft scenes through to the composer each night.

During the development and shoot of the film, transiting Ixion was semi-sextile my ASC, enabling my self-expression. And it was also sextile my natal Ixion, which is the opening flow of the Ixion cycle, showing that I was in a phase where I had

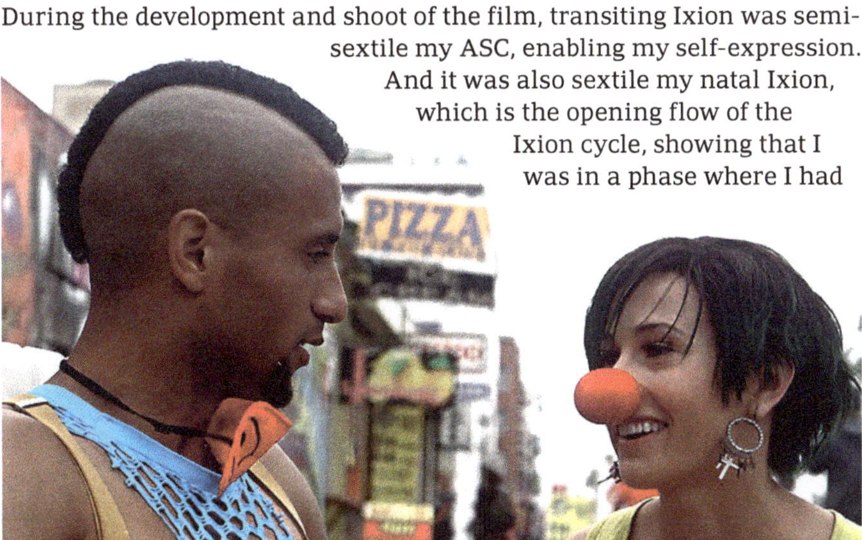

Name: ♂ Alan Clay
born on Su., 7 November 1954
in Wanganui, NZ
175e03, 39s56

Time: 9:26 a.m.
Univ.Time: 21:26 6 Nov.
Sid. Time: 12:08:25

Type: 2.GW 0.0-1 17-Feb-2026

Natal Chart (Method: Web Style / Placidus)
Sun sign: Scorpio
Ascendant: Capricorn
Transits 12 Apr. 2014

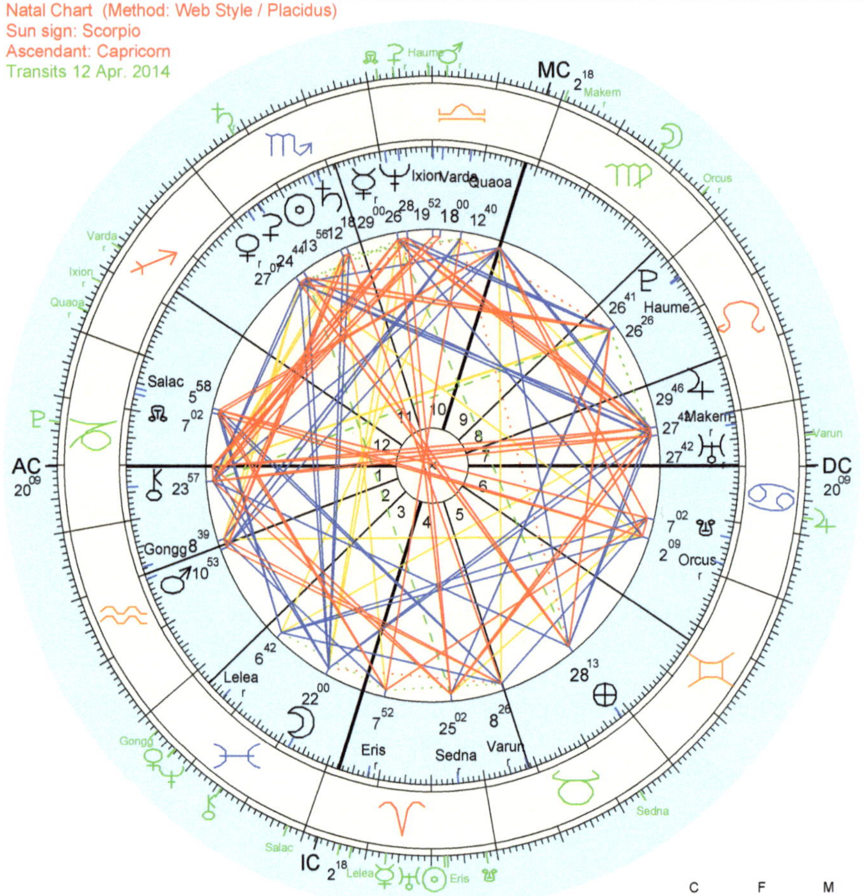

	Natal	Transit
☉ Sun	13 Sco 56'16"	22 ♈ 1'
☽ Moon	21 Pis 59'57"	13 ♍ 8'
☿ Mercury	29 Lib 0'12"r	7 ♈ 41'
♀ Venus	27 Sco 6'49"r	6 ♓ 35'
♂ Mars	10 Aqu 52'40"	17 ♎ 45'r
♃ Jupiter	29 Can 46'16"	12 ♋ 30'
♄ Saturn	12 Sco 18'17"	22 ♏ 2'r
♅ Uranus	27 Can 42' 7"r	13 ♈ 1'
♆ Neptune	26 Lib 28'11"	6 ♓ 42'
♇ Pluto	26 Leo 40'46"	13 ♑ 35'
☊ True Node	7 Cap 2'13"	28 ♎ 24'
☋ Desc.T.Node	7 Can 2'13"	28 ♈ 24'
⚷ Chiron	23 Cap 56'42"	15 ♓ 43'
⊕ P.Fort.	28 Tau 12'58"	not av
⚳ Ceres	24 Sco 43'49"	25 ♎ 55'r
225088 Gonggong	8 Aqu 39'14"	2 ♓ 50'
120347 Salacia	5 Cap 58'14"	27 ♓ 20'
174567 Varda	18 Lib 0'19"	16 ♐ 19'r
541132 Leleakuhonua	6 Pis 42'26"r	5 ♈ 51'
136199 Eris	7 Ari 52'10"r	22 ♈ 30'
136108 Haumea	26 Leo 26'26"	20 ♎ 33'r
28978 Ixion	19 Lib 52'11"	22 ♐ 5'r
136472 Makemake	27 Can 42'14"r	29 ♍ 27'r
90482 Orcus	2 Can 9'12"r	4 ♍ 17'r
50000 Quaoar	12 Lib 39'53"	26 ♐ 46'r
90377 Sedna	25 Ari 2'12"r	23 ♉ 41'
20000 Varuna	8 Tau 26'28"r	24 ♋ 42'

AC: 20 Cap 9'17"	2: 10 Aqu 1'	3: 3 Pis 6'
MC: 2 Lib 17'42"	11: 8 Sco 37'	12: 16 Sag 58'

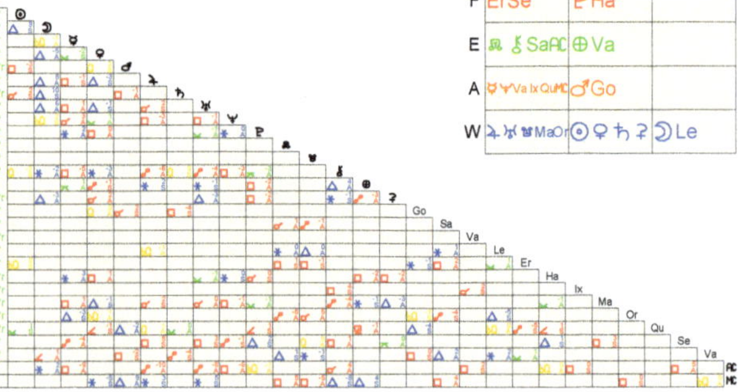

	C	F	M
F	ErSe	♇Ha	
E	☊ ⚷SaAC	⊕Va	
A	☿♆Va IxQuMC	♂Go	
W	♃♅☋MaOr	☉♀♄⚳	☽Le

incorporated this authentic seeker consciousness into my life and was able to follow my bliss in my modern clown work.

The following year the film won Best Comedy at the Hollywood Reel Independent Film Festival and Best Romantic Comedy at Worldfest in Houston - the oldest independent film festival in the world. It's now available on Prime in the US and on TubiTV worldwide.

When the film won the best romantic comedy award at Worldfest, on the 12th April 2014, our new planet of unity consciousness, Haumea, was closely conjunct my natal Ixion. Haumea connects us to the magic of being alive, and to the oneness of our existence. She brings rejuvenation into our lives and can bring about a rebirth. So, the award represented a new beginning in the development of my independent seeker consciousness and my ability to follow my bliss.

Meanwhile, transiting Ixion was square my 3rd house Pisces Moon, showing how my developing authenticity was being acknowledged for the sensitive emotional communication with everyone that this Moon placement represents.

Transiting Ixion was also biquintile my natal conjunction of Uranus, Makemake, and Jupiter, my clown adventure point in my 7th house of relationships. The Uranus and Makemake part of this conjunction is exact,

Name: ♂ Alan Clay born on Su., 7 November 1954 in Wanganui, NZ 175e03, 39s56	Time: 9:26 a.m. Univ.Time: 21:26 6 Nov. Sid. Time: 12:08:25	 Type: 2.GW 0.0-1 17-Feb-2026

Natal Chart (Method: Web Style / Placidus)
Sun sign: Scorpio
Ascendant: Capricorn
Transits 1 July 2017

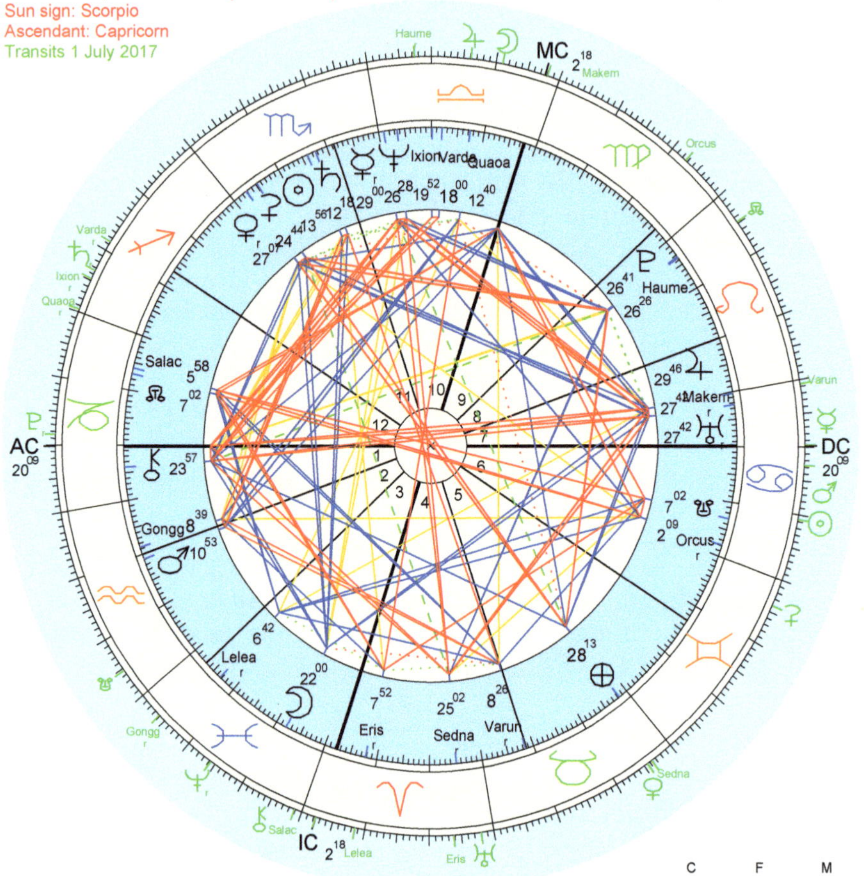

	Natal	Transit
☉ Sun	13 Sco 56'16"	9 ♋ 22'
☽ Moon	21 Pis 59'57"	8 ♎ 57'
☿ Mercury	29 Lib 0'12"r	20 ♋ 21'
♀ Venus	27 Sco 6'49"r	25 ♉ 38'
♂ Mars	10 Aqu 52'40"	17 ♋ 20'
♃ Jupiter	29 Can 46'16"	13 ♎ 53'
♄ Saturn	12 Sco 18'17"	23 ♐ 23'r
♅ Uranus	27 Can 42' 7"r	28 ♈ 5'
♆ Neptune	26 Lib 28'11"	14 ♓ 12'r
♇ Pluto	26 Leo 40'46"	18 ♑ 21'r
☊ True Node	7 Cap 2'13"	25 ♌ 18'd
☋ Desc.T.Node	7 Can 2'13"	25 ♒ 18'd
⚷ Chiron	23 Cap 56'42"	28 ♓ 52'
⊕ P.Fort.	28 Tau 12'58"	not av.
⚳ Ceres	24 Sco 43'49"	26 ♊ 1'
225088 Gonggong	8 Aqu 39'14"	3 ♓ 50'r
120347 Salacia	5 Cap 58'14"	2 ♈ 17'
174567 Varda	18 Lib 0'19"	18 ♐ 33'r
541132 Leleakuhonua	6 Pis 42'26"r	8 ♈ 31'
136199 Eris	7 Ari 52'10"r	23 ♈ 50'
136108 Haumea	26 Leo 26'26"	22 ♎ 38'r
28978 Ixion	19 Lib 52'11"	24 ♐ 41'r
136472 Makemake	27 Can 42'14"r	1 ♎ 54'
90482 Orcus	2 Can 9'12"r	7 ♍ 23'
50000 Quaoar	12 Lib 39'53"	29 ♐ 32'r
90377 Sedna	25 Ari 2'12"r	26 ♉ 28'
20000 Varuna	8 Tau 26'28"r	29 ♋ 26'

AC: 20 Cap 9'17"	2: 10 Aqu 1'	3: 3 Pis 6'
MC: 2 Lib 17'42"	11: 8 Sco 37'	12: 16 Sag 58'

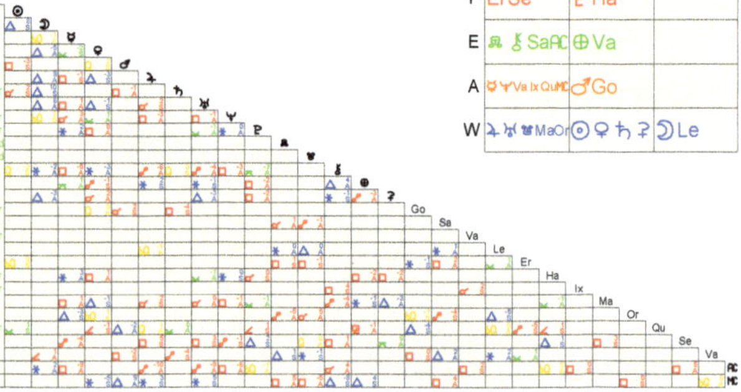

	C	F	M
F	ErSe	♇Ha	
E	☊ ⚷ SaAC	⊕Va	
A	☿♆Va IxQuMC	♂Go	
W	♃♅☋MaOr	☉♀♄⚳	☽Le

and I see Makemake as the higher octave of Uranus, lifting his intuition into a great spiritual understanding. I believe that it is this conjunction that enables me to bring the understanding of these new planets into our collective consciousness, and it also enabled me to research the rich nature of the clown art form.

The conjunction to Jupiter adds opportunity to this understanding, which is why I call this conjunction my clown adventure point. So, the biquintile from transiting Ixion as the film won awards, was an evolutionary flow between my clown adventure and my developing seeker consciousness.

Sedna Consciousness

We might imagine from the previous examples that Ixion is all about clown, which is far from the truth. That is just how this lawless passionate energy has been a blessing in my life but now let's look at the transits for the period during my early Sedna work.

The transiting Haumea conjunct my natal Ixion that I was having as *Courting Chaos* won awards, enabled a more spiritual expression of my seeker consciousness, which brought my astrology work to the fore. Haumea is the Hawaiian goddess of rebirth, and she enables rejuvenation in our lives. I'd worked with Astrology since my early twenties, but during 2016 and 17, I researched and wrote my first astrology book, *Sedna Consciousness, the Soul's Path of Destiny.* This was a huge work because I looked at case studies of all of Sedna's aspects with both the inner planets and with the trans-Neptunian planets, so this also meant researching all the other dwarf planets.

Sedna is our soul consciousness and her placement in our chart tells us what our soul really wants to do in this life. She is always trying to get us onto the spiritual path, and when we are unconscious of her energy, she sends us transcendent crises to help us let go of our old consciousness framework and transcend to a new one. As we step up to

do the soul-based work that we are here to do, we move through a fated transcendence to a more transpersonal consciousness. At the top level we learn to embrace our spiritual destiny and joyfully do what our soul wants to do, and this brings us transcendent peace and the ability to allow love and harmony and nurture abundance.

We find Ixion hard at work in my life during this research period, transiting exactly trine to my natal Sedna, at the time that transiting Sedna was exactly biquintile my natal Ixion. The writing of the book was very fulfilling on a soul level, I knew I was doing the work that I was here to do.

We saw that when *Angels Can Fly* was published, transiting Ixion was in an approaching sesquiquadrate with my natal Sedna, and transiting Sedna was in a close inconjunct with my natal Ixion. During the period of my Sedna research, these had morphed into a trine and a biquintile, so the fated challenge of publishing *Angels Can Fly,* became the spiritual enablement of *Sedna Consciousness.*

Meanwhile, transiting Ixion was sextile my natal Neptune, while transiting Neptune was biquintile my natal Ixion, bringing my spiritual consciousness into play and giving me a vision to articulate.

Transiting Ixion was also biquintile my Jupiter and semi-square my Mars, talking of the opportunity inherit in the project, but also of all the work involved.

And finally, transiting Ixion was quintile my Leleakuhonua, our new planet of multidimensional consciousness, in my 3rd house. Leleakuhonua has recently replaced Sedna as the new outer limit of our solar system, and it is named after a flock of migratory birds from the Hawaiian creation chant, so it talks of the soul growth mission that we are all on together. Astrology is a practise that we collectively develop, and each of our efforts adds to that body of knowledge. So, the quintile from transiting Ixion to my natal Leleakuhonua enabled me to follow my bliss in my Sedna research and play my part in the growth of our astrological knowledge.

Here is a review of the book by Mary Plumb, published in the Mountain Astrologer Magazine.

Alan Clay is in the early wave of astrological pioneers drawn to investigate the dwarf planet Sedna, named after the Inuit goddess of the sea. His comprehensive biographical and astrological research comes together in this unusual book — a collection of life stories and experiences from the "weird new outer limit of our consciousness which is stretching our concepts of reality and is pulling us to look at ourselves as part of the very big picture."

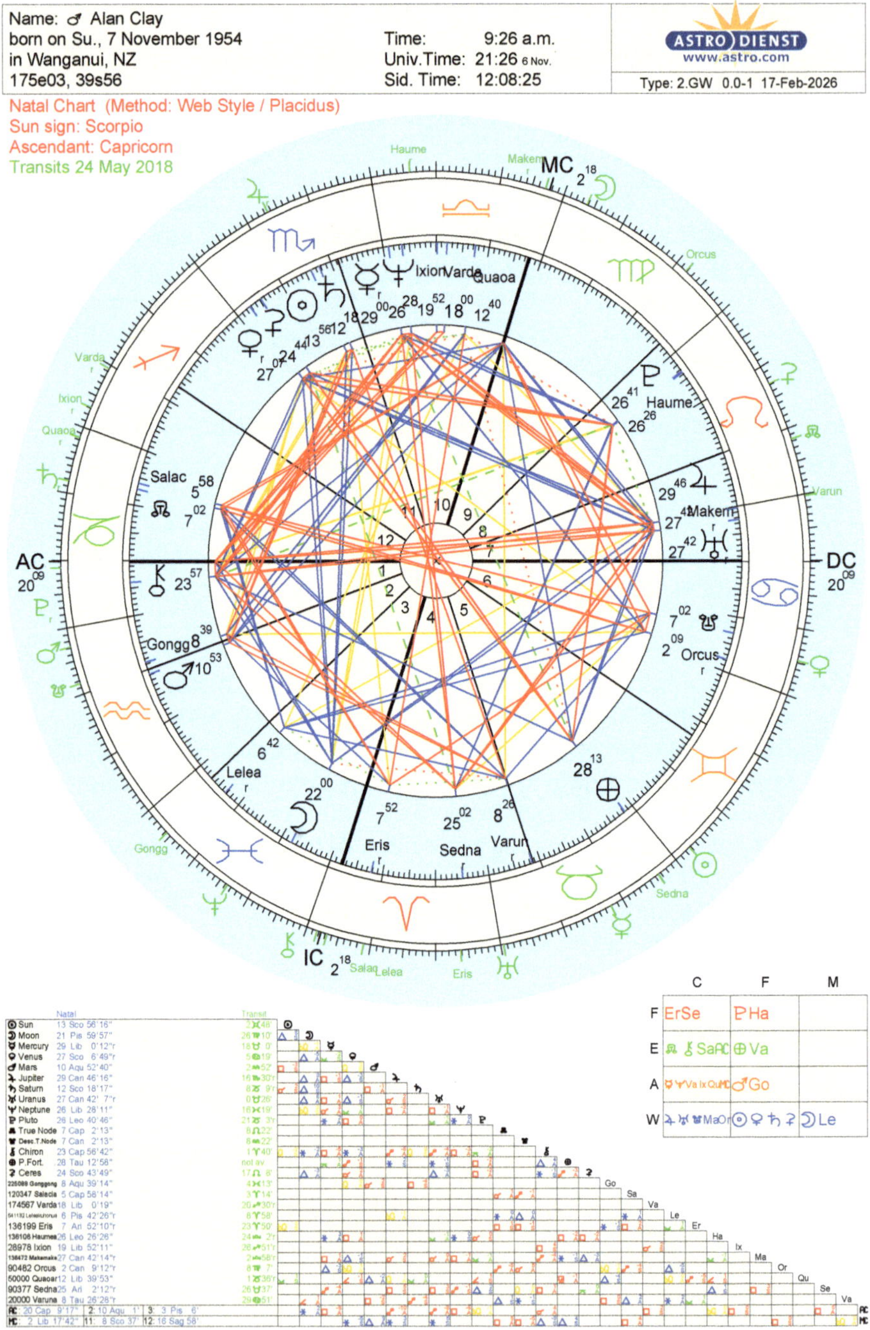

Name: ♂ Alan Clay born on Su., 7 November 1954 in Wanganui, NZ 175e03, 39s56	Time: 9:26 a.m. Univ.Time: 21:26 6 Nov. Sid. Time: 12:08:25	 Type: 2.GW 0.0-1 17-Feb-2026

Natal Chart (Method: Web Style / Placidus)
Sun sign: Scorpio
Ascendant: Capricorn
Transits 24 May 2018

	Natal	Transit
☉ Sun	13 Sco 56'16"	2♊48'
☽ Moon	21 Pis 59'57"	26♍10'
☿ Mercury	29 Lib 0'12"r	18♉0'
♀ Venus	27 Sco 6'49"r	5♋19'
♂ Mars	10 Aqu 52'40"	2♒52'
♃ Jupiter	29 Can 46'16"	16♏30'r
♄ Saturn	12 Sco 18'17"	8♑9'r
♅ Uranus	27 Can 42' 7"r	0♉26'
♆ Neptune	26 Lib 28'11"	16♓19'
♇ Pluto	26 Leo 40'46"	21♑3'r
☊ True Node	7 Cap 2'13"	8♌22'
☋ Desc.T.Node	7 Can 2'13"	8♒22'
⚷ Chiron	23 Cap 56'42"	1♈40'
⊕ P.Fort.	28 Tau 12'58"	not av
⚳ Ceres	24 Sco 43'49"	17♌8'
225088 Gonggong	8 Aqu 39'14"	4♓13'
120347 Salacia	5 Cap 58'14"	3♈14'
174567 Varda	18 Lib 0'19"	20♐30'r
541132 Leleakuhonua	6 Pis 42'26"r	8♈58'
136199 Eris	7 Ari 52'10"r	23♈50'
136108 Haumea	26 Leo 26'26"	24♎2'r
28978 Ixion	19 Lib 52'11"	26♐51'r
136472 Makemake	27 Can 42'14"r	2♎58'r
90482 Orcus	2 Can 9'12"r	8♍7'
50000 Quaoar	12 Lib 39'53"	1♑36'r
90377 Sedna	25 Ari 2'12"r	26♉37'
20000 Varuna	8 Tau 26'28"r	29♋51'

AC: 20 Cap 9'17"	2: 10 Aqu 1'	3: 3 Pis 6'
MC: 2 Lib 17'42"	11: 8 Sco 37'	12: 16 Sag 58'

	C	F	M
F	ErSe	♇Ha	
E	☊ ⚷ SaAC	⊕ Va	
A	☿♆Va Ix QuMC	♂Go	
W	♃♅☋MaOr	☉♀♄⚳	☽Le

Launch at UAC

The book was launched at the United Astrology Conference in Chicago on the 24th May 2018, when transiting Ixion was sextile my natal Mercury-Neptune conjunction in my 10th house. This is my writing point, so my developing seeker consciousness was flowing with my professional inspirational writing. And it was semi-sextile my Venus in the 11th house, so also flowing with my values and relationships in the collective consciousness as I sold the book at a booth in the trade show.

Transiting Ixion was also at the midpoint of my Saturn square Mars, closely semi-square to both, as my developing seeker consciousness challenged me to be responsible and fight the good fight to promote the book. We've seen how Ixion and the clown work has played a big part in releasing the tension in this natal square, and the semi-squares at UAC show that the launch was the result of that work.

Transiting Ixion was also inconjunct my Uranus-Makemake conjunction, so in a fated relationship with my intuitive understanding of the world and my place in it. We've seen how this conjunction enables me to incorporate the dwarf planets into astrological tradition, and the inconjunct at UAC says that the launch of *Sedna Consciousness* was a fated part of my developing seeker consciousness. I was nervous about my reception as a little-known astrologer, but I found that the astrological community was hungry for the new research.

Meanwhile transiting Quaoar, our new planet of spirit consciousness, was closely quintile my natal Ixion. Quaoar talks about a practise that brings spirit into matter, and as one astrologer said, the good reception came about because I was working in tune with spirit. And transiting Jupiter was semi-sextile my natal Ixion, also referencing the opportunity that the conference provided and the good reception the book received.

Also transiting Varda, our new planet of inspiration consciousness, was sextile my natal Ixion. Varda kindles the starlight in the mythology of *the Lord of the Rings* and is much loved by the elves for this light-bringing ability. So, as *Sedna Consciousness* was launched at UAC, my developing light-bringing ability was flowing with my seeker consciousness and talking of the hope and inspiration that the book was bringing.

Sedna was still biquintile my natal Ixion, as it was during the writing of the book, showing the evolutionary opportunity for my soul-growth that both the writing and the launch of the book represented.

And, during this whole period, transiting Ixion was trine my natal Pluto, while transiting Pluto was square my natal Ixion. Pluto is all about empowerment at the top level and so the publication empowered my independent astrological seeker consciousness and put me on the astrological map.

Dwarf Planet University

Following UAC I started teaching online courses on Sedna and then on some of the other dwarf planets, and on the 20th December 2020, I founded the Dwarf Planet University. It was founded under the Jupiter-Saturn conjunction on an election date recommended by Chris Brennan and Leisa Schaim, and the foundation chart has the Jupiter-Saturn conjunction on the ninth house cusp of higher education.

On that date the transiting North Node was trine my natal Ixion, showing that the launch was part of my destined seeker consciousness work. And transiting Venus was closely semi-square my natal Ixion, which tells us that authentic values and relationships would be central to the work.

In the courses students onboard the consciousness of each planet by studying them in their personal chart. What they love is the community sharing through the blog posted assignments and the interactive Zooms, which gives a good picture of how these new planets act similarly, yet diversely in each of our lives.

Meanwhile Ixion was transiting closely inconjunct my natal Jupiter, showing that the Uni was a fated opportunity to expand my work. And it was closely semi-square my natal Sun, indicating that the courses would

Name: ♂ Alan Clay		
born on Su., 7 November 1954	Time: 9:26 a.m.	
in Wanganui, NZ	Univ.Time: 21:26 6 Nov.	
175e03, 39s56	Sid. Time: 12:08:25	Type: 2.GW 0.0-1 17-Feb-2026

Natal Chart (Method: Web Style / Placidus)
Sun sign: Scorpio
Ascendant: Capricorn
Transits 20 Dec. 2020

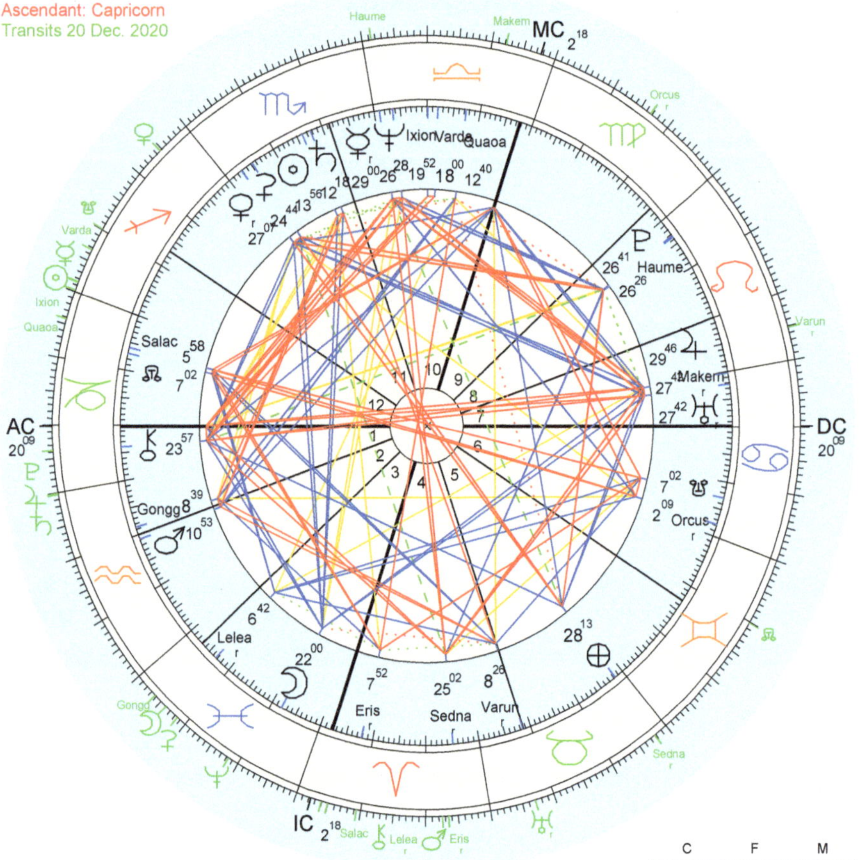

	Natal	Transit
☉ Sun	13 Sco 56'16"	28 ♐ 33'
☽ Moon	21 Pis 59'57"	6 ♓ 2'
☿ Mercury	29 Lib 0'12"r	28 ♐ 29'
♀ Venus	27 Sco 6'49"r	5 ♐ 24'
♂ Mars	10 Aqu 52'40"	22 ♈ 34'
♃ Jupiter	29 Can 46'16"	0 ♒ 6'
♄ Saturn	12 Sco 18'17"	0 ♒ 18'
♅ Uranus	27 Can 42' 7"r	7 ♉ 0'r
♆ Neptune	26 Lib 28'11"	18 ♓ 17'
♇ Pluto	26 Leo 40'46"	23 ♑ 48'
☊ True Node	7 Cap 2'13"	19 ♊ 53'
☋ Desc.T.Node	7 Can 2'13"	19 ♐ 53'
⚷ Chiron	23 Cap 56'42"	4 ♈ 57'
⊕ P.Fort.	28 Tau 12'58"	not av.
⚳ Ceres	24 Sco 43'49"	8 ♓ 27'
225088 Gonggong	8 Aqu 39'14"	3 ♓ 45'
120347 Salacia	5 Cap 58'14"	3 ♈ 56'
174567 Varda	18 Lib 0'19"	23 ♐ 19'
541132 Leleakuhonua	6 Pis 42'26"r	9 ♈ 24'r
136199 Eris	7 Ari 52'10"r	23 ♈ 30'r
136108 Haumea	26 Leo 26'26"	28 ♎ 38'
28978 Ixion	19 Lib 52'11"	29 ♐ 46'
136472 Makemake	27 Can 42'14"r	7 ♎ 47'
90482 Orcus	2 Can 9'12"r	13 ♍ 13'r
50000 Quaoar	12 Lib 39'53"	4 ♑ 12'
90377 Sedna	25 Ari 2'12"r	27 ♉ 48'r
20000 Varuna	8 Tau 26'28"r	4 ♌ 49'r

AC: 20 Cap 9'17"	2: 10 Aqu 1'	3: 3 Pis 6'
MC: 2 Lib 17'42"	11: 8 Sco 37'	12: 16 Sag 58'

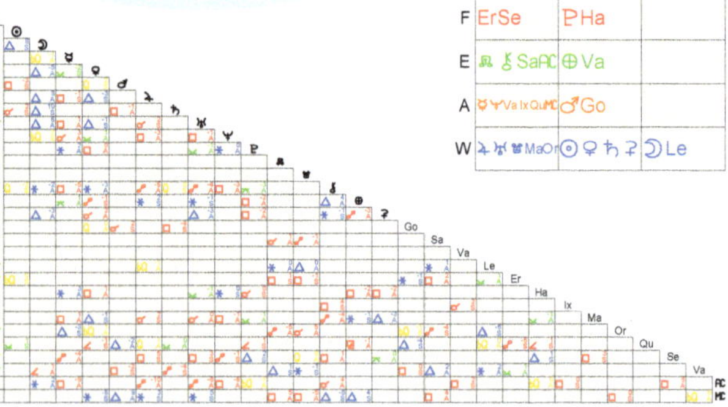

	C	F	M
F	ErSe	♇Ha	
E	☊ ⚷ SaAC	⊕Va	
A	☿♆Va IxQuMC	♂Go	
W	♃♅☋MaOr	☉♀♄⚳	☽Le

be central in developing my seeker consciousness. Ixion was transiting conjunct my Sun as I started teaching clown, and it was in the opening semi-square as I created the vehicle for my astrology teaching.

Transiting Ixion was also closely sextile my natal Mercury in the 10th house as the Uni was launched, enabling the professional communication of my independent seeker consciousness through the courses and the talks on the dwarf planets.

And finally, transiting Ixion was closely quintile my natal Varda, our new planet of inspiration consciousness, in my 10th house. Varda gives us the ability to create light in times of darkness, and this transit shows that the Uni would provide a deep opportunity to integrate my developing seeker consciousness with my ability to shine a light in my profession and bring hope and inspiration to the students.

These new planets represent new aspects of consciousness that are coming available to us and through the courses we see that simply by making these new aspects conscious, students become empowered and their lives are transformed. The empowerment of this process is addictive and so they are eager to return for more. As a result, all the courses have a wonderful mix of ongoing students and newcomers.

Ixion in the Signs

So let's look at how Ixion has manifested in the signs. As we've just seen, I am part of the Ixion in Libra generation.

Ixion in Libra

Ixion was in Libra from 1934 to 1965. Those born with this placement are part of the first generation to experience the "Generation Gap', where the children had a very different view of their lives than their parents. This comes from Libra's focus on relationships and Ixion's passionate individual approach. Ixion is always asking 'are the rules we're playing by the right ones?' and those of us born with Ixion in Libra didn't accept our parent's rules.

We're the generation who later in life started having de facto relationships rather than getting married... something that was scandalous to the older generation. We are also the first to believe in personal values, accepting as natural that each person can have their own values, and that we don't have to simply accept the collective values around us.

And in the justice system we are the reformers, pioneering the idea that laws need to be updated for the current time. Prior to this, law was built on tradition, new laws were introduced which built on the older laws, but older laws were seldom if ever repealed.

Ixion in Scorpio

Ixion was in Scorpio from 1965 to 1996. This period saw an increased interest in the occult and in magical practices. And because Ixion brings a passionate individual approach and Scorpio is all about relationship, this was a period of sexual and social liberation, with the early 1970s seeing the growth of the modern lesbian and gay movements.

And because each transit highlights the opposite sign, in this case Taurus, we had the 'greed is good' movement in the eighties, epitomised by the movie Wall Street. The lead character celebrated in this film, Gorden Gecko, is a very unconscious Ixionic character, essentially a sociopath who is out for whatever he can get.

Those of us born with Ixion in Scorpio will reflect these themes. We are attracted to the occult and to magical practices. And we value freedom and individuality in our relationships, but, when we are operating at the inner planet level of consciousness, we might be too self-involved to be sensitive to the unspoken agreements on how far we can go.

As we develop spiritually, we likely have a passionate approach to our esoteric studies which enables a deep and unique investigation of these topics. And we find an unashamed authenticity in our relationships by learning to follow our heart and to ask for forgiveness when we cross the line.

Ixion in Sagittarius

Ixion was in Sagittarius from 1996 to 2021. This period was marked by a heightened sense of freedom and individual rights and a growing sense of the inevitability of these rights. So in Sagittarius he was overthrowing preconceptions and encouraging radical philosophies as well as conspiracy theories and fake news.

Alongside this has gone a freedom-of-belief approach to spirituality, so Ixion in Sagittarius has seen the birth of pluralism, the acceptance that we can each believe what works for us. But this has also created the fervent fundamentalist backlash that we saw at the end of this cycle. A lot of us have simply gone along with the crowd on pluralism, without really accepting the validity of anything other than our own view.

Those of us born with this placement will therefore be fierce defenders of our personal freedom and we will have a passionate curiosity about the world. We are able to follow our bliss in our philosophical understanding of our lives and be authentic in our spiritual work. However, we have to be careful of immersing ourselves in bubbles of media and friends that simply support our current view.

Ixion in Capricorn

Ixion went into Capricorn in 2021 and the goal of this transit, I suggest, is to adjust our systems so each of our individual approaches can flourish within the collective. Ixion does this by taking action and asking for forgiveness afterwards, rather than permission before, so we can see the widespread taking advantage which is occurring in the form of corruption and even the rise of criminal regimes. In this period, we are likely to see all the loopholes in the system being exploited and the system itself likely being perverted by the criminal actions of leaders and of people from all walks of life.

Yet at the same time these pressures will motivate us to strike out in search of new ways of governing ourselves and new systems and institutions which can be put in place to foster individuality within the system. The end result of this is likely to be greater individual freedom within society for each of us to pursue our passions.

And the opposition to Cancer suggests that in reaction to this there could also be a 'return to family values' pushback against the likely evolving diversity and decentralisation of social structures in this period.

Ixion in the Houses

We see the ethereal energies of the outer planets manifesting most clearly in our personal lives through their house position. The houses each represent a different area of our lives and they focus a planet's energy and give it the space in which to play. If you don't know your Ixion house placement, the next chapter in this book explains how to work out where Ixion and the other dwarf planets are in your chart.

First House

At all levels, with Ixion in the 1st House we are likely to embody this independent energy in our essence. We feel that it is important to do what we want, when we want and to honor our own compass. And we learn that the more authentic we can be, the more resourceful and adaptable we will be, and the better our life works.

This is the house of our early development, and with this placement we could have experiences in childhood that push us to develop our authenticity and set us off on our passionate mission to be ourselves. We could also develop defense mechanisms, where we willfully follow our personal desires as a way of protecting ourselves from what we feel is the exploitation of others.

At the unconscious level, our impulsive independence can be problematic because Ixion was a loner in myth who was shunned by society for his lawless ways and so themes of breaking or bending the law, or of ostracism can manifest in our lives if we are not consciously working with the energy.

As we get onto the spiritual path however, this placement enables an independent spiritual investigation. Although many spiritual practices require submission and acceptance to a higher master, we must have the room to be ourselves and make the practice our own. At this level our seeker consciousness has an awareness of the spoken and unspoken rules inherent in our interactions, and we are able to catalyze social change.

Like Clara Barton, who was a trailblazing nurse who worked in hospitals during the American Civil War and later founded the American Red Cross. She wanted to create an organization dedicated to humanitarian aid in times of crisis, and this revolutionized disaster relief efforts.
At a time when women didn't even have the right to vote, her leadership

challenged societal norms by promoting women's active engagement in philanthropy and social change, contributing to the advancement of gender equality.

At the top level, this placement can give a unique sense of self, together with an awareness of the social norms within which that uniqueness is embedded. As we learn to follow our spiritual bliss, we develop a passionate vitality in our work. Our seeker consciousness becomes central in all our experience, and we can center in this awareness. At this level we can lead the way by example and play a unique role in shaping the future.

Like German-born physicist, Albert Einstein, who is famous for his Theory of Relativity, which postulated that all observation is dependent on the observer. This is a very Ixion in the 1st House perspective. This theory revolutionized our understanding of space, time, and the fundamental laws of physics by introducing the concepts of curved spacetime and time dilation. It paved the way for advancements in technology, such as GPS, as well as furthering our understanding of the universe and the possibilities of time travel.

Second House

Ixion in the 2nd House gives an inner strength to pursue what may well be a rocky financial road. It encourages unconventional finances and many with this placement may end up working for themselves. The more authentic we can be in our attitude towards wealth and material possessions, the more self-worth we will feel and the more faithful we will be to our independent values.

At the unconscious level, however, we are likely to play fast and loose with the resources at our disposal, by not paying our bills, or cutting financial corners, getting involved in confidence schemes, or deceiving through nondisclosure, or through straight-out theft. At this level we may also be seduced by sensual pleasures.

Once we get on the spiritual path with this placement, we may be able to make a considerable amount of money, so long as that is the result of our individual spiritual passion. The more generous we are, the more successful we will be. But we may also lose resources and maybe respect at some point, and, when we accept this and learn from it, we will be able to make the most of our second chance.

Like Swami Chidvilasananda, also known as Gurumayi, who is an Indian spiritual teacher and leader of the Siddha Yoga path. She oversees a wealthy ashram with substantial donations and assets. However, the movement was rocked by leadership controversies and scandals involving her predecessor and brother, and, as a result, attendance dropped and she faced challenges to her authority. However, she remained leader after the scandals and reoriented the movement, continuing to teach and adapt, attracting new followers.

At the top level, Ixion in the 2nd House can bring an inspired understanding of how to work in the physical world to enable our personal freedoms and thereby effect change from within. At this level, we have a practical seeker consciousness and may set up social rules to assist this process or develop disruptive technology which encourages this independence. Our unorthodox philosophy and the uncompromising, direct style of its likely presentation, might generate a measure of allure or notoriety which assists the reach of our work.

Like UG Krishnamurti, an Indian non-academic philosopher, who questioned enlightenment. He rejected the very basis of thought and in doing so negated all systems of knowledge. Hence, he explained his assertions were experiential and not speculative. *"Tell them that there is nothing to understand."* Although many considered him an "enlightened" person, he often referred to his state of being as the "natural state". He claimed that the demand for enlightenment was the only thing standing in the way of enlightenment, if it existed at all.

Third House

With Ixion in the 3rd House, we will be free thinkers. No-one is going to tell us what to think or believe and we will likely challenge established thought in some way. We may appear to know things in advance of others, and by the time everyone else catches up, we are on to something else, so we may be underestimated and overlooked.

At the unconscious level, this placement can bring undesirables into our lives as siblings or neighbors, who push us to develop our freethinking approach. We might also get caught in thinking patterns and be prone to gossip and bad mouthing or trash talking people in our neighbourhood. This placement can also arouse some willful righteousness in our communications with others, which may alienate them and turn them into enemies. As we grow, owning the 'bad' boy or 'bad' girl inside of us will lessen the need for this energy to be projected and to manifest as other people.

As we develop spiritually, our seeker consciousness is enabled, and we learn to follow our bliss in our ideas and our esoteric research. At this level, we find all of our communication to be a valuable learning process, and this enables us to clearly formulate our thoughts and express our passionate independent ideas. While we feel the need to be accepted by those with a more traditional approach, we can find the courage to challenge this orthodoxy by expressing ourselves and asking for forgiveness afterwards rather than permission before.

Like English naturalist, geologist, and biologist, Charles Darwin, whose Theory of Evolution through natural selection, changed our perspective on the world. He was raised in a freethinking family and studied medicine but gave it up to become a fanatical naturalist. Yet he struggled with the contradiction between the prevailing Christian religious beliefs and his scientific findings, only publishing his book *Origin of the Species* later in his life.

At the spiritually evolved level, this placement brings an evolutionary power to chart a new course for humanity with our ideas and through our communication. We find that we are able to make the connections that are important for us and we have the mental dexterity to ensure that all of our interactions become valuable opportunities to promote our view. At this level, our seeker consciousness can catalyze the development of society through the pursuit of our independent ideas.

Like Polish astronomer and author, mathematician, and Catholic canon, Nicolaus Copernicus, who formulated a model of the solar system that placed the Sun rather than Earth at its centre. In his 1543 model, the Earth rotates on its access each day and the planets revolve around the Sun. And this is still how we still look at it today, so he is the founder of modern astronomy.

Fourth House

With Ixion in the 4th House, our home will be a unique expression of who we are and hospitality, or the absence of it, will be central in both our birth home and in the home that we create as an adult. With this placement the pressures and experiences that we have in our family and in our home-life will push us to develop an independent psychological foundation which gives us an inner emotional security. So, the more authentic we can be, the more comfortable and secure we will feel.

At the unconscious level, however, this placement can bring undesirables into our home, and these people could be guests or other family members. We all start life unconscious, so childhood can be the time when these undesirable people and experiences come into our lives to push us to develop our independent streak. If we are still experiencing this as adults, it is important to remember that if we don't own the planetary energies ourselves in every moment, we experience them in projected form.

As we develop spiritually, we learn to create a sacred space which provides a base for our developing seeker consciousness. By working through the karmic baggage that we brought with us into this life, we develop an authentic spiritual approach. Our ability to 'follow our bliss' through adversity in our personal lives becomes an inspirational public example that is likely to both bring us the respect and support of society and keep us safe from any ongoing conflict or controversy.

We see this in Pakistani female education activist, Malala Yousafzai, who was shot by the Taliban on her way to school for her passion to learn, and for speaking out about the rights of women to education. Her family relocated to England to facilitate her recovery and protect her from further attack, and she has gone on to win the Nobel Peace Prize and become a leading human rights campaigner.

At the spiritually evolved level with this placement, our home becomes our temple, and our personal story becomes archetypal. The provocative experiences that we have, particularly when we are young, will push us to develop our spiritual authenticity. At this level, we can create an authentic sacred space where our karmic challenges empower our seeker consciousness and inspire others.

Like the Dalai Lama, who is the foremost spiritual leader of the Tibetan people. Born in a farming family in a small village, he was discovered at the age of 2 by the search team looking for the new incarnation of the Lama. However, he was held for ransom several times on his way to the capital. Then later, when China invaded Tibet, he was forced to flee to Nepal. Despite these difficulties, his followers are inspired by his resilience, forgiveness, and unwavering commitment to the principles of love and compassion. This message has resonated with people around the world, and he has become a revered world leader.

Fifth House

With Ixion in the 5th House, we will have a unique way of loving, and we will likely have love affairs which fall outside the norm and allow us to explore ourselves. Or we could have children who play fast and loose with the rules and push us to develop a unique parenting approach. Or we could be creative in a willfully independent and avant-garde way.

At the unconscious level, we have to be careful of becoming infatuated or obsessed with someone, in the hope that they will reciprocate those feelings. And, if we are not embodying the 'bad' boy or 'bad' girl energy of the planet ourselves, we may experience love affairs with people who may turn out to be not what they originally seemed and, in the extreme, may even be sociopaths, or draw us into illegal situations. At this level we could also be prone to risk-taking and, if we are not sensitive to the financial limits or the real market situation, we could lose money through gambling or speculation.

Like English mathematician, cryptologist and philosopher, Alan Turing, who posited that intelligence and consciousness are not exclusive to human minds and could potentially be replicated in machines. He is famous for what is now known as 'the Turing test' which evaluates a robot's ability to exhibit intelligent behaviour that is indistinguishable from that of a human. He is credited with formalizing the concepts of algorithm and computation with his Turing Machine which broke the German code during WW2, making him the father of computers and AI. However he was convicted of homosexuality when he reported to police that his male lover had stolen valuables.

As we develop spiritually however, this placement gives us a playfulness which enables our seeker consciousness. The joy of this facilitates our developing authenticity, as we learn to enjoy being ourselves. At this level we have both the creativity and the contemplative perspective required to learn from our experience and so we are able to make the most of any second chances we may receive, which encourages our experimental approach.

Like American performance artist, musician and filmmaker, Laurie Anderson, who specializes in multimedia projects focusing on the use of language, technology, and visual imagery. She has consistently evolved by adapting her artistic practice throughout her career, demonstrating a willingness to learn and grow. She continues to challenge herself creatively and to receive critical acclaim for her innovative and thought-provoking performances.

At the top level our individual creative efforts can resonate so strongly with the collective consciousness that it leads to meaningful change. The more we can come from a place of love in this work, the better it will function. The rich story world that we create, or the unique real-world event or product we manifest, provides a frame or context for others to see and develop the uniqueness in their own lives.

Sixth House

With Ixion in the 6th House, we will have a uniquely personal approach to wellness and diet that works for us. We are able to fill our days by following our passion in each moment and, in so doing, develop our own unique daily routine. This is the house of the services we provide, and, over time, we may be able to provide an original outside-of-the-box service.

At the unconscious level, however, we are likely to rebel against the pressure to conform in our routine or our job. At this level our attempts to develop an individual routine can be a reactive process of cutting corners and bending the rules where possible. If confronted and offered a second chance, it will likely be wasted, which can eventually lead to an outcast status. Again, we might project the energy, if we don't embody it ourselves, and then we are likely to find shady characters inhabiting our daily routine in some way.

When we're on the spiritual path we learn to turn our daily activities into spiritual rituals and we might engage in voluntary work, if it gives us the opportunity to follow our passion. At this level, the more authentic we can be, the more strength and vitality we feel. We understand that every moment gives us a chance to be authentically ourselves, and that when we act on this awareness we can connect with the divine.

Like Indian spiritual leader, Bhuteshananda, the head of the Ramakrishna movement, who encourages devotees to integrate their daily activities, such as work and service, into their spiritual practice. He believes that by engaging in acts of service with a selfless and compassionate attitude, it not only benefits others but also helps us to purify our own heart and mind. He encourages his followers to see work as a spiritual duty, performed with dedication, sincerity, and ethical values.

And at the top level, this placement can give our seeker consciousness an individual service mission. We have the courage to be ourselves and an ability to see through the detail of each moment and connect with the big picture. This can create a uniquely individual spiritual approach that enables us to help others who are on their own journey or looking for something similar.

Like Swiss astrologer, Louise Huber, who, together with her husband, is known for her development of a unique psychological approach to astrology called the Huber Method. This approach views people as active participants in their own lives rather than solely influenced by celestial bodies. It sees astrology as a tool for self-awareness and personal development, which can uncover the deeper psychological motivations and patterns behind astrological configurations, and offers insights into personality traits, life purpose, and potential areas of growth.

Seventh House

With Ixion in the 7th House, we will have passionate one-to-one relationships that can run outside the bounds of social norms. By being sensitive to the unspoken agreements with our partners, we are able to make the space to be authentically ourselves. And, as we learn to co-operate and share with others, our seeker consciousness is enabled. With this placement we can see where we can bend the rules in our negotiations, and how to find the holes in our contracts.

At the unconscious level, however, we might feel more like a victim in this process, getting caught in the contract loopholes. Or we might be actively trying to exploit these loopholes. We could also feel like we have to take any steps necessary to maintain our relationships, even potentially illegal actions. Or we might experience this in projected form and find ourselves in relationships with shady characters. Either way, at this level, we may find that these relationships do not give us the freedom we need.

This is exemplified in the theories of American behavioral psychologist, B F Skinner, who considered free will to be an illusion. He saw behaviour as solely a result of reinforcement and conditioning, with no regard for internal mental processes, subjective experience, or individual agency. Because there is no room for free will or personal autonomy, his view is criticised as denying individuals the ability to make conscious choices and actively shape their own behaviour.

When we are on the spiritual path, we learn to be diplomatic and co-operative in our one-to-one relationships, while maintaining our authenticity. We understand that we must live for something we feel passionate about even within the bounds of our relationships. This placement enables us to develop our seeker consciousness through unique one-to-one relationships that assist us in following our bliss and in doing our spiritual practice.

At the spiritually evolved level, Ixion in the 7th House understands the unspoken agreements in relationships that enable them to work. This placement blesses each of our relationships with a missionary like focus, together with a playful irreverence to the norms, which enables them to be the vehicle of our unique contribution. At this level, we will transmute our base emotions and may even forswear couple relationships because of a 'marriage to God'.

Like Florence Nightingale, who established the first secular nursing school in the world and is considered the founder of modern nursing. She perceived her calling to nursing as a divine mission, seeing it as a way to serve God and alleviate the suffering of others. She believed that her dedication to her work required her to forgo personal relationships and the pursuit of a conventional family life. She made a vow of chastity and saw this as a sacrifice she willingly made in service to her calling.

Eighth House

With Ixion in the 8th House of the occult and sensitivity to the spirit world, we will have a unique take on the deep mysteries of life. We can see beneath the relationship drama in our lives and understand how we can follow our bliss in those interactions. With this placement we will not be content living under someone else's thumb and will need to strike out for our independence sooner rather than later.

At the unconscious level however, we may cut corners and take advantage of the joint resources we hold with others. At this level we can have a passionate desire to fulfill our base emotional needs, with little regard for the effect this has on others or our relationships. Or we might experience this in projected form, where others use us for their pleasure. But this is the house of debt and judgement, so it is really important that we learn from the mistakes that we make as we play out the drama of our lives.

As we develop spiritually, our seeker consciousness is strongly enabled by this placement in the house of self-transformation. We will likely have a passionate interest in the spirit world, in the occult, or in astrology. At this level we are able to deal with the karma of this house and learn from our mistakes. This enables an authenticity that brings freedom and regeneration into our lives.

This ability to play with the drama of our lives is exemplified in the work of Lucille Ball, one of the greatest female clowns in history. She became well known through her sitcom *I Love Lucy*, of which she was both the star and producer. Her mischievous and impulsive nature drove much of the comedy, and the show often highlighted the contrast between her aspirations and the realities of daily life.

At the spiritually evolved level this placement brings an ability to adopt a playful approach to weighty occult issues. We can follow our bliss through the cycles of deaths and rebirth. The openness of this approach gives us a sort of clairvoyance, enabling us to see how the energy is likely to flow and situations evolve. At this level, we can enable a cross-fertilization of approaches into a new independent approach, so that a new best practice emerges.

Like Dane Rudhyar, who was a French-born American astrologer. He was the founder of humanistic astrology, which brought together traditional astrology and Jungian psychology. This centered the interpretation in the growth of the person, rather than in the determinative effect of their life, a perspective that revolutionized modern astrology. He introduced and popularized many astrological concepts that were previously unfamiliar or less explored, and his willingness to challenge traditional astrological methods attracted people who were looking for new perspectives and approaches.

Ninth House

Ixion in the 9th House can bring a passionate personal exploration of a topic that is close to our heart. We are searching for the meaning of things, and we know how to play by the rules and also where they don't make sense and need to change. As a result, we may have an independent philosophical approach to life. And, as we develop our personal passion, we may write, talk, teach, or lead others in a unique way.

At the unconscious level however, we may be more interested in bending the rules to our own advantage. Or we could be too emotionally invested in our personal passion and, as a result, cut corners. We might proceed without authorization, or act illegally in some way, because we feel that 'the end justifies the means'. However, it doesn't in most instances, and so we may run into a confrontation with the authorities as a result. There is also a danger that we may not learn from these experiences and may repeatedly cut corners, or get led astray by our base emotions, leading to stronger and stronger consequences.

As we develop spiritually, however, this placement enables us to follow our spiritual bliss as we embark on a path where we learn from our mistakes. At this level our seeker consciousness develops by charting our own course through the traditional spiritual philosophies, taking on board what works for us from each discipline. We have independent dreams and visions which may be motivated by seemingly disruptive events in our lives. These encourage our authenticity and, as we rise to the occasion, we are likely to find that our individual life mission may also inspire others.

Like Helen Keller, who became blind and deaf as a one-year-old. This gave her a truly unique mission to express herself, as she grew from a child who knew no words, could not hear others, and could not even see their lips moving, to someone who could write and even speak publicly. She became a linguist, a motivational speaker and a writer, authoring 14 books and touring the world, giving talks which were an inspiration to many.

At the top level, this placement brings an understanding or a wisdom which is born of our authenticity and enables us to manifest our dreams and visions. Failures or setbacks are seen as learning experiences, so second chances are maximized. Our unique 'far out' thinking, coupled with an ability to communicate this unique perspective, enables us to become thought-leaders. As a result, we may get involved in publishing, broadcast media, or social media, or take on the role of teacher or moral leader.

Like Mohandas Gandhi, who was an Indian lawyer who led a campaign of nonviolent resistance against British rule. He used fasting as a tool to mobilise people and pressure the British government. By subjecting himself to physical hardships, he showcased the contrast between the ideals of nonviolence and the repressive actions of the British government. His fasts were powerful forms of protest that aimed to draw attention to specific grievances or injustices, and his leadership and moral authority inspired people to join his movement.

Tenth House

With Ixion in the 10th House, we are likely to feel that we don't fit in the box being offered by society, and we need to learn to make our own way in the world. Over time, we will create a unique social position that allows us the freedom to be ourselves and act as a catalyst for the development of new social norms.

At the unconscious level, however, this placement encourages us to get what we want in society without thought to the consequences. If we are in the thrall of our base emotions, this can lead us into some tricky, even illegal, situations. This is particularly true in our professional relationships where we may not respect the implicit agreements that underpin them and so act disrespectfully or try to take advantage in some way.

As we embark on the spiritual path and begin to transmute our base emotions, we learn that anything is possible, but not always right now. Our seeker consciousness develops through trial and error in our professional interactions, and we learn where the limits are in each situation so we can maximize these. And we also discover where we can break from tradition and foster our authenticity.

Like American comedian Harpo Marx who was known for developing his unique stage and screen persona largely through experimentation. He began as a speaking performer but, after an audience's poor reaction to his voice, he decided to never speak on stage again, creating his famous silent, pantomime character. His act often involved pushing and breaking social and comedic norms. He maximized his onstage potential specifically by knowing when and how to deviate from tradition. By cultivating his nonverbal persona, Harpo broke from comedic tradition and created a form of performance that was truly authentic to himself, embracing his strengths and unique comedic style.

At the top level with this placement, we can become leaders in our chosen field. We will likely approach our work with reverence, and there will be a corresponding reverence for it from the public. We may even become seminal influencers and inspire others to follow in our footsteps and chart their own course.

Like Dion Fortune, who was a highly influential occultist, mystic, and novelist in early 20th-century Britain. Her approach to spiritual and esoteric work was marked by deep reverence, particularly through her founding of the Society of the Inner Light. She also inspired reverence from her followers and became a central figure in modern Western esotericism. Her books are seen as seminal in the development of many occult and modern magical traditions. Fortune is openly acknowledged as one of the truly foundational leaders in her field, with many others drawing upon her teachings to develop their own practices. Her pathbreaking work established her as both a leader and inspiration to countless spiritual seekers.

Eleventh House

With Ixion in the 11th House, we have passionate hopes and ambitions, and we want to be free to follow our heart. This is the house of collective consciousness, so we value community and Ixion's placement here drives us to seek out groups where we can play a unique role or have the space to be ourselves. We are consciously, or unconsciously, always tuning into the human weather pattern around us and sensing what is allowable in this particular gathering of people.

At the unconscious level however, we might play fast and loose with the people we know through our profession. We may be so seduced by wealth that we take advantage wherever we can and in the extreme we may get involved with shady activities. If we do, we are likely to believe that because we have got away with it until now, we will always get away with it, so we learn nothing from experience.

Once we are on the spiritual path, however, this placement brings the same passion and willful independence to our exploration of consciousness, likely gaining both support and controversy from the community in the process. This is the house of self-realization and here our seeker consciousness develops through experience, which may include periods of feeling like an outcast because of our independent approach. The more charitable we can be in our social interactions the better this will work.

Like Alexandria Ocasio-Cortez who is the Democratic Congresswoman for the Bronx and Queens areas of New York City. With Ixion in the 11th House, she has a lawless collective consciousness mission. Elected at age 29, she is the youngest woman ever to serve in the United States Congress.

She is very progressive in her views and advocates for the Green New Deal, Medicare for All, a jobs guarantee, free public college and the abolition of U.S. Immigration and Customs Enforcement.

At the top level with this placement, we can make a unique and valuable contribution to the collective consciousness, challenging established norms and entrenched ideas and systems. At this level, by coming from a place of love, we are able to follow our personal bliss. This authenticity may enable us to bring a bold new vision of who we are and what unites us and so become leaders in consciousness.

Like American futurist, inventor, and author, Ray Kurzweil, well known for his ideas on artificial intelligence and transhumanism, which have inspired new ways of thinking about consciousness and our interconnectedness. He has presented a bold vision of the potential for human enhancement through technological advancements in biotechnology, artificial intelligence, genetic engineering, and nanotechnology. He believes that by integrating technology into our bodies and minds, humans can transcend their current limitations and evolve into a "posthuman" state.

Twelfth House

With Ixion in the 12th House, we will have a unique spiritual view and are likely to question the spiritual orthodoxy. With this placement our authenticity is our hidden talent, and the more we foster this, the more we can see through the fog of conformity that we find around us. Following our bliss is an intuitive process and we are able to preserve our freedom of action by asking for forgiveness when we cross the line.

At the unconscious level, we might find we are living largely independent lives which are however alienated from a society which is omnipresent and seems to be always working against us. And we might set up this alienation by not respecting the implicit agreements in our relationships and by not learning from experience. Or we may be too passionately invested in our own point of view and be too unconsciously blinkered to see what is really happening around us. This is the house of prisons and institutions, so there may be real world consequences for going too far, but we may also be able to find a refuge.

Like Australian hacker and activist, Julian Assange, who founded Wikileaks. He was accused by two women of rape. Then by the United

States for conspiring to publish classified material on his website. He sought refuge in the Ecuadorian Embassy in London for 9 years and was subsequently in prison for 5 years in the UK fighting extradition, before being released on bail after striking a plea deal to plead guilty to a single felony charge. This allowed him to return to Australia as a free man after considering his time served.

Once we get on the spiritual path and start clearing our unconscious spiritual baggage, however, this placement gives us a rich field of activity for our spiritual growth. As we work through our karmic debts, we likely have ongoing spiritual realisations. This allows our seeker consciousness to develop through a trial-and-error approach where failures are simply seen as learning experiences. At this level, our seeker consciousness is able to seed the zeitgeist and change the world.

Like Ada Lovelace, an English mathematician and writer who assisted in the design of the first mechanical general-purpose computer, the Analytical Engine, almost 200 years ago. The machine was never built, but she is considered to be the first computer programmer because she developed the algorithm to explain how the machine would do its various calculations. In a letter to her mother when she was working on it, she said that she was "pre-eminently a discoverer of the hidden realities of nature" and she claimed to have "an intuitive perception of things hidden from eyes, ears & the ordinary senses."

At the spiritually evolved level, this placement can bring an almost direct connection with the divine. We can become a channel, and the divine can manifest through our uniquely independent approach to the material world. By being bravely ourselves, we discover miracles, and by following our bliss we enable abundance. At this level our unashamed authenticity brings healing into the collective unconscious.

Workbook to Onboard Ixion in Your Life

1. Work out where Ixion is in your birth chart:

    a. Go to www.astro.com and create a free account.
    b. Then choose "Extended Chart Selection" under "Charts & Data" and put in your birth data.
    c. On this data screen, at the bottom on the left under 'Additional Objects', you can choose to include the dwarfs, which are listed as Asteroids, and you do this by highlighting them. The dwarfs in this box are *Ceres, Eris, Haumea, Ixion, Makemake, Orcus, Quaoar, Sedna & Varuna.*
    d. Then opposite this, in the box on the bottom right, add these numbers (225088,120347,174567,541132) to also include *Gonggong, Leleakuhonua, Salacia & Varda.*
    e. Click 'Show the Chart' to see it.
    f. Then click 'Additional Tables' at the top left of the chart to get the table of positions and aspects.

2. Look up the house interpretation in this book for your house placement and see what resonates.

3. What does the Sabian Symbol for your Ixion indicate to you? Search online for Dane Rudhyar's or Marc Edmund Jones's interpretations. (Remember to round up to find the right symbol, i.e. 22.04 = 23).

4. Next, understand how Ixion interacts with the other planets in your chart by studying the aspects. I.e. – is Ixion conjunct, opposite, trine, square or sextile any of your personal planets or points like Sun, Moon, Ascendant, Mercury, Venus, Ceres, Mars, Jupiter or Saturn? How about the transpersonal planets like Uranus, Neptune, Pluto, Eris, Orcus, Salacia, Quaoar, Makemake, Gonggong, and Sedna?

5. Choose a significant moment of understanding in your life and look up the transits of Pluto and Saturn to your natal Ixion on that date. You can find the list of where these two planets on this ephemeris: https://www.astro.com/swisseph/swepha_e.htm. And then check the Ixion transits to your other natal planets. You can find the Ixion ephemeris at this link:

6. Given what you've learned so far, write a couple of paragraphs on how can you best activate Ixion in your life.

Ixion's Place in our New Firmament

The outer planets represent aspects of consciousness. We have become familiar with Uranus, Neptune and Pluto, and over the early years of this century we have discovered 12 new planets who offer us a rich feast of new consciousness. Let's look at each of these outer planets to put them in context.

As we embark on the spiritual path to make a larger sense out of the experiences of our personal lives, we start activating our Uranian and Neptunian energies and bring them into our consciousness. As we do, we begin to realize that the 'you can't take it with you" approach of the inner planets is actually a delusion.

Uranus brings intuitive flashes into our personal planet consciousness and begins to connect us with the collective consciousness, breaking through our Saturnian defences to allow new impulses and connections. So, the discovery of Uranus enabled consciousness growth in our lives. We can look at Uranus as the higher octave of Mercury because he takes Mercury's ideas, communications and curiosity, and networks them at a higher spiritual level.

Neptune tunes us into the bigger picture and brings spiritual consciousness into our lives. He encourages us to search for a larger meaning for our personal experiences and teaches us about faith as a way of deepening consciousness. Neptune is traditionally considered to be the higher octave of Venus, where the inner planet's values and aesthetics are expressed at a more spiritual level through the imagination and psychic opening of Neptune.

Which brings us to dwarf planet **Pluto**, who is the start of the outer transpersonal planets. Here we must accept the limitations of the ego consciousness, let go of compulsions and unconscious constructs and accept that change is the only constant. Pluto is traditionally considered to be the higher octave of Mars.

The discovery of Pluto enabled the psychological understanding of our lives. This produced the shadow paradigm, where the darkness in our souls is seen to be buried in our unconscious, and the convenience of this is that we don't have to address it on a day-to-day basis. But we need to ditch Pluto's shadow paradigm to enable him and these other new energies consciously in our lives. As with all the other outer planets,

Pluto manifests differently depending on our level of consciousness, so what we have been calling his shadow is simply his manifestation when we are at personal planet consciousness.

As we get on the spiritual path, Pluto gives us an adaptability and resilience which enables us to mediate the transition occurring in our lives in each moment. And at the spiritually evolved level, we can transmute loneliness and separation into love and long-term relationships and effect a regeneration in our lives.

Pluto now has two new brothers who share his orbit and his angle to the ecliptic. They also share his gravitational resonance with Neptune, as all three do two orbits of the Sun, to every three of Neptune's. These brothers are however polar opposites.

The first is **Ixion**, who encourages us to be a passionate, but lawless, follower of our heart, or loins, depending on our consciousness level. He's always asking the question: 'are the rules we're playing by the right ones?' And he does this by pushing the boundaries and asking for forgiveness afterwards, rather than permission before. As we develop a spiritual approach, we can learn to honour the bad girl or bad boy energy inside us and follow our heart. At this level Ixion encourages us to be an independent and unique expression of ourselves, while being sensitive to the unspoken agreements in our relationships, so we know how far we can go.

The second is Pluto's straight-talking brother, **Orcus**, our new karmic consciousness. He is the master of integrity at the highest level, but he also encourages us to engage in double-talk and deception at the personal planet level. Yet as we develop spiritually, he gives us a self-sufficiency that will nourish us through the long and difficult work that we sometimes find necessary, plus a capacity to deal with the shadow side of our lives. At this level we become accountable for our deeds and actions. We learn to align with a spiritual creed and understand the karmic process of life. And, at the highest level, we gain the shamanic ability to transmute shadow into light.

Next, we have **Salacia**, our new higher-love consciousness, who gives us a self-protective quality that helps us weather both the physical and the psychic storms in our lives. She can give us the power to foresee opportunities and find the appropriate time to embrace them. She enables us to take a leap of faith, especially when we know we are going to be profoundly transformed by the experience. At the personal planet level there can be erotic fascination or interest, and we might engage in socially unacceptable, even illicit, sexual activity. As we develop spiritually, she brings a light-heartedness that enables our psychic intimacy with others and can bring popularity. At the highest level, Salacia is about bringing true love into our lives and empowering us spiritually.

Then we have **Varuna**, our new mastery consciousness, who is the higher octave of Saturn. Where Saturn rules by control and through laws and restriction, Varuna has a natural sovereignty, but we have to claim this through action. Sovereignty is a dance between our intention and the collective psyche. We have to claim it and at the same time others have to agree to give it to us. We start this process by stepping forth in some way and saying, 'I can do this'. And then we have to keep doing it over time. And, when we do, we gain support and notability for this work. Once we are on the spiritual path, Varuna teaches us to stand in the centre of our lives and own the results of our dance of karma and dharma.

As we move further out from the Sun, we find **Haumea**, our new unity consciousness, who is a creation deity of the Hawaiian people. She is both an earth goddess and a fire goddess, and she represents regeneration and rebirth. She is the higher octave of Neptune, turning his psychic opening into real psychic connection. At the personal planet level however, this can manifest as a lack of connection, a sort of spiritual alienation. As we develop spiritually, she provides a link with the oneness of humanity, with the magic of being alive. So, she represents a direct link with the soul level when we can open ourselves to it, and, as we deepen this connection to Source, we learn to facilitate a constant psychic renewal in our own lives and in the lives of others.

Just beyond Haumea, we have our first non-gendered planet, **Quaoar**, our new spirit consciousness. Quaoar is the creation deity of the Tongva people, who are indigenous to Los Angeles. Quaoar sings and dances the world into existence, so this planet talks about a practice of bringing spirit into matter. Singing and dancing are practices that bring spirit into matter, and so are yoga, meditation, walking in the woods, and many other things. Anything can be a practice to bring spirit into our lives. We can look at Quaoar as the higher octave of Jupiter. Where Jupiter is a sort of dumb luck, Quaoar turns each moment into a dynamic meditation where we can see the opportunities and act on them in real time, so Quaoar is like smart luck.

Our next planet is **Makemake**, opening us to the new richness of systems consciousness, which gives us a worldview built from our experience, and a view of our place in that world. He is a spiritual trickster, enabling us to innovate and to play with the area of life signified by his position in our natal chart. He gives us a devotional focus that borders on genius and encourages us to see ourselves as an organic whole, as well as a member of a team. We can look at him as the higher octave of Uranus, lifting Uranus' intuition into a rich understanding of life. At the personal planet level, we might use this rich intuitive understanding to hide in plain sight, to blend into the background as a safety mechanism. As we develop spiritually however, he calls spiritual nourishment into our lives and gives us a devotional focus bordering on genius.

Then we have **Varda**, our new inspiration consciousness. Varda is the much-loved Elven goddess from *The Lord of the Rings*, who kindled the starlight. She enables us to win our battles with the dark forces through hope and inspiration, and she can lead us through a transition to a new state of being. She's all about finding the light in our lives or shining our light in the world. So, she enables us to navigate the "dark night of the soul" or any other "dark" confusing time. She trains us to be more objective, more careful, more aware of whole situations — and less impulsive and intent upon side issues. And she supports us to walk away from previous betrayals and associations and encourages us to look towards new horizons and start afresh elsewhere.

This is followed by **Gonggong**, our new empathic consciousness, who encourages us to participate in the marketplace of life. He is an psychic wizard at the highest level, enabling us to feel inside other people and walk a mile in their shoes. We have to get out of our own emotions to empathize with others however, so at the personal planet level, he can be a bit of an enfant terrible, encouraging us to be emotionally self-indulgent and to lash out in an attempt to get our own way. As we develop spiritually, we understand that we live in a symbiotic relationship with others, and that our divine work is to let go of our own base emotions so we can be sensitive to the emotional community in which we are nestled and open to the empathic support of others. This empathy allows us to motivate others from the inside, to combine our energies and lift the spiritual vibe.

Next, we have **Eris**, our new diversity consciousness, who is the warrior sister of Mars in myth. And we know that Pluto is the higher octave of Mars, so Eris is the higher octave of Pluto. She shines her fierce grace on everything in our lives, seeking inclusion and validation for all the disparate facets of our psyche. At the personal planet level, she encourages us to engage in discord and strife, so we learn to stop fooling ourselves, or stop being fooled. But as we adopt a more spiritual approach, she enables us to see clearly without preconceptions and keep our body and mind in harmony so that health and happiness prevail. And at the highest level she is a spirit-guide, transmuting life into love.

Then we make a big jump to **Sedna**, our new soul consciousness, who has an orbit of over eleven thousand years. Sedna is always trying to get us onto the spiritual path. She represents *Our Soul's Path of Destiny* because, if we accept that our soul incarnates over a number of lifetimes and that it has a purpose to grow through these incarnations, then in this life, that purpose is shown by the Sedna placement. She is always trying to get us onto the spiritual path, and when we are unconscious of her energy, she sends us transcendent crises to help us let go of our old consciousness framework and transcend to a new one. As we step up to do the soul-based work that we are here to do, we move through a fated transcendence to a more transpersonal consciousness. We learn to embrace our spiritual destiny and joyfully do what our soul wants to do, and this brings us transcendent peace and the ability to allow love and harmony, and nurture abundance.

And finally, we come to **Leleakuhonua**, our new multi-dimensional consciousness, who talks of the soul growth mission that we are all on together. Leleakuhonua has an orbit 5 times as large as Sedna, so it steps Sedna's soul consciousness up to become a unified soul-field, where, at the top level, we can see our soul reflected in the other souls in our lives. This planet teaches us to be both independent and interdependent at the same time, and it talks about the huge missions we have to undertake to make a change in our lives so that we can better sustain ourselves. This planet gives us extrasensory abilities, where we can 'read the field' on a level which is far greater than just picking up the sensory cues, and this includes precognition. Our soul knows it's journey and the more we can tap into our higher selves and be sensitive to the signals from our soulmates, the better we will be able to orient ourselves on our big collective soul-growth mission.

Dwarf Planets as Higher Octaves

Here is a framework of higher octaves to help us understand several of the dwarf planets. A higher octave expresses an inner planet energy at a more spiritual level and so gives us one way to understand these new bodies.

But Dane Rudhyar reminds us in this quote from Horoscope Magazine, that the higher octaves also act on the lower octaves to repolarize and transform them.

> *When Uranus, Neptune and Pluto are considered as "higher" expressions of such planets as Mercury, Venus and Mars… the closer planets are seen to represent a "lower octave" of biological-personal functions or energies; the more remote ones, beyond Saturn, a "higher octave" constituted of more transcendent and "spiritual" activities or qualities of being.*
>
> *There is some truth, no doubt, in such statements if one restricts oneself to a consideration of only the external events of a person's life. The "illuminations" which Uranus may bring to the consciousness that is not frozen into Saturnian rigidity can inspire and transform the Mercury mind. The compassion and inclusiveness which are characteristic of Neptune do act directly — if allowed by Saturn so to act—upon the sense of value and the feeling-judgments represented by Venus. The power of inescapable destiny and total surrender to a cause, which defines essentially Pluto's operations, do transform — if allowed to do so — the strictly personal initiative of Mars.*
>
> *But the essential fact is that the activities of Uranus, Neptune and Pluto run counter to the normal functions of Mercury, Venus and Mars. The former are not just personal activities of a "higher" kind; they are activities meant to disturb and transform — indeed, utterly to repolarize and reorient those of Mercury, Venus and Mars.*[4]

So, with that in mind, here is a higher octave framework for some of our new dwarf planets. (The planets in bold are dwarf planets).

4 https://www.khaldea.com/rudhyar/astroarticles/planetaryoctaves.php

Sedna - **Ceres** - Moon
Haumea – Neptune – Venus
Makemake – Uranus – Mercury
Eris – **Pluto** – Mars
Quaoar – Jupiter
Varuna - Saturn

We can think of **Sedna** as the higher octave of **Ceres**, who is our newly reclassified inner dwarf planet. Ceres is our ability to love and be loved. At both a basic level and in the bigger sense of the word, she represents what we need to feed and nourish ourselves. And we can think of Ceres as the higher octave of the Moon. The Moon is our emotional center, mediating our survival moment to moment, and Ceres mediates our survival over time. Sedna steps this heart-centered energy all the way out to the new limit of our solar system, so she talks of our survival over lifetimes. Here we learn to let go of the physical realm and allow transcendence to a new holistic spiritual consciousness where we can allow love and harmony, and nurture abundance.

We can see **Makemake** as the higher octave of Uranus, which in modern astrology is the higher octave of Mercury. Makemake gives Uranus's intuitive impulses meaning and context, which transforms our understanding of his unexpected ways. And Uranus's lateral web gives Mercury's detail an energetic network to organize and connect his information. All three planets are tricksters, and Makemake is a spiritual trickster who allows us to experiment with the area of life signified by his position in our chart.

We can think of **Haumea** as the higher octave of Neptune, where Neptune's psychic opening has the potential to blossom into real psychic connection with Haumea, a connection to the soul level. Neptune is traditionally considered to be the higher octave of Venus, echoing her values and aesthetics at a higher spiritual level. We see a love of beauty and a belief in values in all three of these bodies.

In mythology **Eris** is the warrior sister of Mars, and in our lives, where Mars is fighting mundane battles, Eris' challenge is on a more esoteric level. In modern astrology **Pluto** is considered to be the higher octave of Mars, so we can look at Eris as the higher octave of Pluto. She steps up his transformative energy to a fierce grace through which everything in our lives is opened to the light and can be transmuted into love.

We can look at **Quaoar** as the higher octave of Jupiter. Both planets talk of expansion and of new possibilities, but where Jupiter expands through a mix of luck and a hunger for more, Quaoar repolarizes Jupiter so we can see the new opportunities and deftly take the appropriate action to enable the expansion that is possible in each moment. Where Jupiter is a sort of dumb luck, Quaoar turns each moment into a dynamic meditation, where we can see the opportunities and act on them in real time. So, Quaoar is like smart luck.

And we can think of **Varuna** as the higher octave of Saturn. Both are supreme rulers, but where Saturn limits, controls, and structures, Varuna transmutes this energy into self-sufficient mastery. However, like Saturn, Varuna can place restrictions on us if we are not being true to ourselves or honest with others, but these dissipate when we forgive and align with Spirit.

Gonggong – **Salacia** – Mars/Venus

I look at **Gonggong** as being the higher octave of **Salacia**, who I see as the higher octave of Venus and Mars combined. If there was a planet that combined Venus and Mars it would be all about relationship and sexuality, and Salacia steps that up to a psychic one-to-one contact, while Gonggong steps that up even further to an empathic contact with an ability to channel psychic and emotional energy.

Ixion – Pluto - Orcus

And finally, Pluto now has two new brothers who share his orbit as well as his angle to the ecliptic. All three are at the same octave level. The two brothers are, however, polar opposites. The first is the seeker consciousness of **Ixion**, who enables us to develop our authenticity. While the second, **Orcus**, opens us to karmic consciousness, teaching us to align with a spiritual creed and understand the karmic process of life.

Dwarf Planet University

The information in this book comes out of research at the Dwarf Planet University, where we are pioneering the astrological exploration of the Kuiper Belt. The dwarf planets speak of new aspects of consciousness that are arising in our lives, and we offer 6-week courses to on-board each of them.

The courses explore the planets in our personal chart and the charts of the other class members. We look at the house placement and the aspects and research our transits, as we understand how to on-board each aspect of consciousness.

The course format mixes webinars, blog-posted assignments and live Zoom Q&As, so you can attend from anywhere in the world. We start with a live Welcome Q&A and we explore the House position in the first fortnight, the aspects in the second and transits in the third. Each fortnight includes an instructional webinar, an investigative assignment based on your personal chart and a live 2 hour Zoom Q&A session.

Assignments are posted on a private forum so we can learn from, and comment on, posts from our fellow course members. And the live Q&A sessions are recorded so we can pick up classes we miss.

The students on our courses range from beginners to very experienced astrologers, and it is this range that is the source of the vibrant class culture. What students love is the community sharing that occurs, through the blog-posted assignments and live Zoom Q&As, which gives a good picture of how these new planets act similarly, and yet diversely, in each of our lives.

We offer a Dwarf Planet Astrology Diploma on completion of any 8 of our 13 courses, but you are also welcome to do courses singly and in any order. All the courses have a mix of ongoing and casual students, which provides a creative cross pollination of experience levels.

What Students Say:

I highly recommend the Dwarf Planets Course for the insights and the amount of new information and perspective gathered. Alan's teaching inspires one and brings new light and spiritual understanding to charts (certainly to mine). His humor and friendly approach made the seminars very enjoyable, yet profound.

Elisabetta Quintiliani - Italy

Alan Clay's sensitive, cutting edge wisdom and the community sharing make the classes on the Dwarf Planets compelling and profound. They are as much an exploration as a revelation. Not only mentally stimulating, they are a deep dive into each of our psyche and growth experience. I love them and am looking forward to more.

Karen La Puma, Astrologer, Counsellor, Speaker

I'm very grateful for Alan Clay's insightfully powerful dwarf planet courses. He offers a supportive and welcoming class environment that encourages learning and processing the deep new consciousness of these planets. I totally recommend engaging with this outer realm of alchemy into our inner self!

Sue Rose Minahan, Evolutionary Post-Modern Astrologer

What Alan Clay has created with the Dwarf Planet University is nothing short of genius. His in-depth knowledge and amazing teaching style are unique and what the astrological world has been waiting for. I'm so enjoying learning about our far-reaching dwarf planets amongst a galaxy of friendly, intelligent student astrologers from all over the universe, logging on at their differing time zones.

Eileen Richardson, UK.

Alan Clay's work has transformed my thinking—about my chart, about my practice—even about astrology itself. Alan is a born teacher.

Ariel Harper Nave, Canada

I absolutely loved the class! As a first-time student of astrology, I can honestly say that aside from Alan (a wonderful teacher and guide), every one of the students in the class was a teacher for me. I learned so much and can't wait for the next class to begin. -

Mary Anne Pitt, USA

Who would have thought that studying the dwarf planets would lead to such an expansive awareness of my soul's journey? For this, I am very grateful. The style and structure of Alan's teaching provides the group with a very warm, safe and informative space in which to learn. I love being part of the group. Thank you, Alan.

Marian Ryan, Energy Therapist, Author, Teacher, UK

As one returning to astrological study after decades away, I find Alan's instruction fun and informative, and the classroom format a gift of shared learning for everyone participating. Alan has created a safe and supportive space where anyone, at any level of knowledge, can thrive and shine. His obvious love of this work illuminates its presentation. I echo the comments of others, "Best astrology classes ever!"

Nalini MacNab, USA

"I have been sensing a reciprocity in my study of the dwarf planets. As I shift focus and embrace each of their unique energies, I am in turn rewarded by a richer understanding of myself and the world in which we live."

Alison Glennie, Ireland

Meet the Writer

A New Zealander, Alan Clay, is a transpersonal astrologer, who specializes in the outer planets. Inspired by the work of Dane Rudhyar, Alan's work has broadened over the years into a study of the new dwarf planets, and today he is one of the Kuiper Belt's astrological pioneers.

For many years, Alan worked internationally as a clown and a clown teacher. He describes clown as being "a big research into people and what makes us human". And he combined this research with astrological consulting to explore the depths and potentials of the human psyche.

Alan's well-known clown textbook, *Angels Can Fly*, includes a mix of clown theory, workshop and street exercises, anecdotes from 20 international clowns, and fictional stories that follow the adventures of 10 street clowns.

He is also the writer and director of an award-winning romantic comedy film, *Courting Chaos*, in which a Beverly Hills girl falls for a Venice Beach street clown called Chaos, and she must overcome her inhibitions and become a clown herself for the relationship to survive.

His novel, *Believers in Love*, tells the story of a father and daughter team of sand-sculptors, who embark on a crazy adventure from Bondi Beach to a magic mountain in New Zealand, exploring the transient nature of art and life, to discover that dreams are real. Reviewers called it *"A book about love, laughter and life. Not just a story, this is an exploration of emotion and philosophy. A novel of journey and self-discovery."*

Alan's first astrology book, *Sedna Consciousness, the Soul's Path of Destiny* was launched at the United Astrology Conference 2018 in Chicago. It is the ultimate reference on Sedna, the new outer limit of our solar system, and includes house interpretations and aspect interpretations with all the traditional planets, as well as the new dwarf planets.

Following several years of teaching dwarf planet astrology courses online, Alan founded the Dwarf Planet University under the Jupiter/Saturn conjunction in 2020. Since then he has developed all the course material that is used by students at the Uni, and he leads the fortnightly live Zoom Q&A's. He still works as a consulting astrologer and is available for chart readings by Zoom.

In 2023 the Dwarf Planet University started publishing a series of textbooks on the new planets. *The Astrology of Haumea, Neptune's Higher Octave* was released in May and *The Astrology of Makemake, Uranus' Higher Octave* in October. These books are co-written by Alan and his assistant, Melissa Billington.

The following year Alan published *New Stars for a New Era: A Consciousness Workbook for our 10 New Planets.* This book includes chapters on Ixion, Orcus, Salacia, Varuna, Haumea, Quaoar, Makemake, Gonggong, Eris and Sedna.

"Alan Clay has written a comprehensive book on the newly discovered dwarf planets, exploring everything from their mythology to practical application. More than just reading about these celestial bodies, Alan shows us how to work with their energies and incorporate them into our lives. Best of all, the book is accessible to both seasoned astrologers and novices eager to gain an understanding of the emergence of new consciousnesses in our world. A strong recommendation for this groundbreaking book."

Armand Diaz, from a review in the NCGR Memberletter

www.ingramcontent.com/pod-product-compliance
Lightning Source LLC
LaVergne TN
LVHW052347100826
845147LV00012B/776

* 9 7 8 0 6 4 5 8 0 3 3 3 4 *